MEET MY WATERLOO

A Midwestern American Boyhood

Written and Illustrated by
Lloyd Engelbrecht

EAGLE EDITIONS
2007

EAGLE EDITIONS
AN IMPRINT OF HERITAGE BOOKS, INC.

Books, CDs, and more—Worldwide

For our listing of thousands of titles see our website
at
www.HeritageBooks.com

Published 2007 by
HERITAGE BOOKS, INC.
Publishing Division
65 East Main Street
Westminster, Maryland 21157-5026

Copyright © 2004 Lloyd Engelbrecht

All rights reserved. No part of this book may be reproduced or transmitted in any form or by any means, electronic or mechanical, including photocopying, recording or by any information storage and retrieval system without written permission from the author, except for the inclusion of brief quotations in a review.

International Standard Book Number: 978-0-7884-2559-2

Dedication

To my treasured schoolmate friends from those innocent years: Mel, Joyce, Bussy, Lu Lu, Tom, Dorothy, Esther, Jimmy, Hoppy, Willis, Gene, Mary Lou, Raymond, Bobby, Toots, Charlie, Evanell, Norma Jean, Patsy, Vernon, Auts, Gloria, Betty Jane, Jean, Joanne, Ruby, LeRoy, Mardell, Pete, Margie, Raymond, Roy, Betty, and Roland.

Acknowledgement

I thank LaVerne Diekemper and Harry Sennott for helping me verify certain facts about our town. I also thank my editor and wife, Molly Engelbrecht, who keeps me from making egregious grammatical errors, and adds class to my writing.

Table of Contents

List of Illustrations	*vii*
Prolog	1

PART I   **The Time and Place**
Chapter 1	Origins of the Town	5
Chapter 2	My Town	11
Chapter 3	My Time	15

PART II   **The Heartbeat of the Town**
Chapter 4	The Tradesmen	23
Chapter 5	The Word Gets Around	37
Chapter 6	Entertainment	45

PART III   **My Education**
Chapter 7	Family	55
Chapter 8	School	63
Chapter 9	Church	69

PART IV   **Home**
Chapter 10	The Kitchen	77
Chapter 11	The Attic	83
Chapter 12	The Cherry Tree	87
Chapter 13	My Shed	91
Chapter 14	The Basement	95

PART V   **Ritual**
Chapter 15	Weekly Ritual	101
Chapter 16	Radio	113
Chapter 17	Tradition	117

Table of Contents (Continued)

PART VI	**Fun**	
Chapter 18	Swimming	125
Chapter 19	The Field	131
Chapter 20	Games and Other Delights	137
PART VII	**Adventure**	
Chapter 21	Trains	145
Chapter 22	Airplanes	159
PART VIII	**Vocation**	
Chapter 23	Growing Up	169

Epilog 175
Endnotes 177

List of Illustrations

Waterloo Skyline	Cover
The Boy - Lloyd Engelbrecht (photograph by Wilbur Engelbrecht)	1
Map of the Mississippi River Valley near Waterloo	5
Waterloo Map	10
Waterloo Skyline	11
WPA Church Street Culvert Project	15
Tradesmen at the "Roger's Seminary" Apartments	23
The Iceman's Order Card	24
Frozen Milk	26
The Switchboard Operators	37
Telephone (circa 1935)	39
The Town Siren	41
The Band Concert	45
Lloyd and Grandma (photograph, photographer unknown)	55
Washington Hall	63
Immanuel Lutheran Church	69
The Kitchen	77
The Attic	83
The Back Yard	87
The Shed	91
The Basement	95
Drying the Laundry	101
Listening to the Radio	113
The Drum Major	117
The Raft	125
The Field	131
Third Street Sledding	137
The Train's Water Stop	145
The Surprise Airplane Adventure	159
The Delivery Boy	169

The Boy - Lloyd Engelbrecht (c1939)

Prolog

The Waterloo Republican published an article telling a legend of how the town got its name. The article[1] reads as follows:

> The origin of the town's name is always an object of deep interest. Waterloo, of course, was named after the town of Belgium, site of Napoleon's defeat by Wellington, but why was that particular name given to this town?
>
> The town was originally divided into two parts---Bellefontaine at the South, named by the French for

the beautiful spring there; and Peterstown at the north, named for Peter Rogers, an early and prominent settler there.

The two communities were divided by a creek which can still be seen along the Harry Jackson property, through Reifschneider's pasture, and through the Koenigsmark subdivision, and there was said to have been intense rivalry between the two towns.

Legend has it that in 1818, a chap by the name of Charles Carroll, an Irishman, came upon the scene, and to the astonishment of the Peterstownsmen and the Bellefontainers, ignored the rivalry and built his house on one side of the creek, his barn on the other, and said, "It won't be Bellefontaine, and it won't be Peterstown, but begorra, I'll give ye's both your Waterloo."

Now I'd like to tell you the story of *my* Waterloo. It is the town of my youth, a place where I made friends, played freely, enjoyed my fantasies, went to school, and, grew up. The stories and the sketches in the following chapters flow totally from my memory, and as you will see, "my Waterloo" is also a set of precious visual and historical recollections. It is my pleasure to share these memories with you and I hope that you enjoy them as much as I have relished recording them in this book. Now -- six decades later -- Meet My Waterloo!

Lloyd Engelbrecht
December 2002

Part I
The Time and Place

Chapter 1   Origins of the Town

Chapter 2   My Town

Chapter 3   My Time

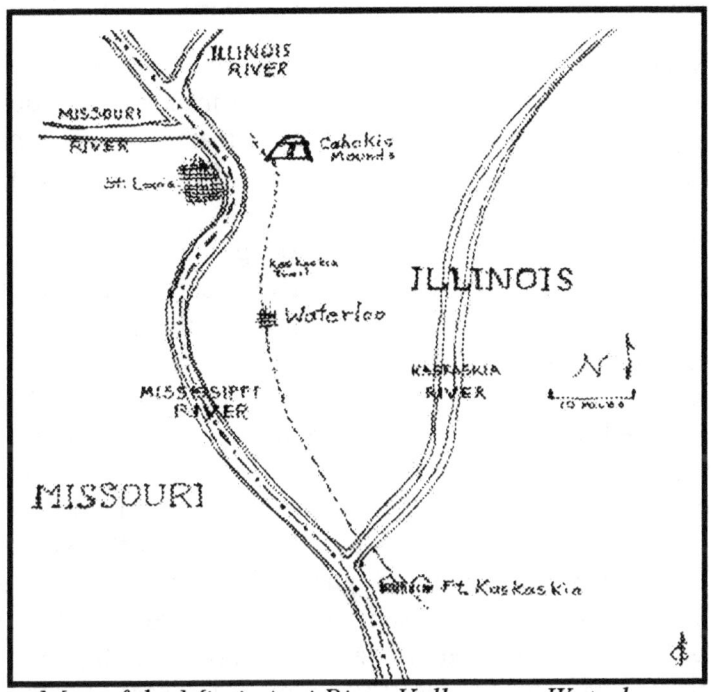

Map of the Mississippi River Valley near Waterloo

Chapter 1   Origins of the Town

Bickelhaupt. Eichelmann. Reifschneider. Matzenbacher.
Zimmermann. Asselmeier. Schulmeister. Koenigsmark.
Brinkmann. Mickenheimer. Hauptfleisch. Quernheim.
Hartmann. Gummersheimer. Osterhage. Schoeneberg.
Burgdorf. Glessner. Wallhaus. Engelbrecht. Hamacher.

Our names shouted our Teutonic heritage! I have little sympathy for those who stumble in the pronunciation of Engelbrecht. As a child, you had to learn the pronunciation of these names because adults were courteously addressed as "Mr. Feldmeier" or "Mrs. Reinhold." If these names could be mastered by a child, everyone could do it. Not that we didn't have some easier names such as Braun, Grosse, Keim,

Meet My Waterloo   *Origins of the Town*

Mueller, Schmidt, and Voss, but the majority of the names were constructed in the complex German style to describe some characteristic associated with that surname. And the majority of the town of my youth was of German descent.

But not always. The territory along the Mississippi River between St. Louis, Missouri and the southern tip of Illinois near Cairo could command access to the majority of the navigable waters between the Appalachian Mountains to the east and the Rocky Mountains to the west. The Spanish explored the area in the early 1500s, but did not settle. It was the French who explored and settled in the late 1600s and early 1700s, and they now guarded all this territory to New Orleans. Fort Cahokia was established across the Mississippi River from St. Louis to guard the access to the upper Mississippi, Illinois, and Missouri Rivers. The upper Mississippi provided trade to territory as far north as Minnesota. The Illinois River provided access to commerce throughout Illinois as far away as Chicago, and the Missouri River permitted travel to the Rocky Mountains in the west. The French also established Fort Kaskaskia to protect the Kaskaskia River watershed in southern Illinois. Finally, the Ohio River joins the Mississippi near Cairo, providing access to the Appalachians, and what is now Ohio, Indiana and Kentucky. It is no wonder that the French felt the necessity for this territory to be protected.

Waterloo is located between Fort Cahokia, about twenty miles to the north, and Fort Kaskaskia, about twenty-five miles to the south. Since the French governed the territory, Waterloo had early French civilian settlers who had traveled with the military forces. The British also recognized the value of the area, and would gain control from the French, bringing with

Meet My Waterloo   *Origins of the Town*

them English settlers. So the French and English were present before the Germans, but they, too, were not the first.

The importance of these water routes was also recognized much earlier in time by Native Americans. The Cahokia Mounds State Historic Site, located at the junction of the major rivers (Illinois, Missouri, and Mississippi), shows evidence of a large population of mound builders whose skill rivaled or exceeded that of the Aztecs.[2] The settlement at the Cahokia Mounds was a huge trade center based on access via the rivers. The Kaskaskia Trail extended southward from the Cahokia Mounds and was part of the trade infrastructure along the Mississippi River. Waterloo is now situated on that trail, which provided its Bellefontaine spring as a necessary replenishment site for residents and travelers alike. The Native Americans were the earliest known inhabitants of the land.

French access to the area was through Louisiana and then northward on the Mississippi River. British forays brought subsequent settlers from Canada. Once the territory was acquired by the United States through the Louisiana Purchase of 1803, control shifted to the U.S. military. Like the French and British, civilian American settlers accompanied the military travelling from the eastern seaboard colonies to military stations in the west. This group, being from the eastern seaboard, were primarily of colonial and English extraction. They journeyed overland across what is now Pennsylvania, Ohio, Indiana, and Illinois, or they traveled on the Ohio and Mississippi Rivers to their destination. Because of the vastness of the land they were occupying, it was often possible for these early settlers to become large landowners.

The years around 1840 saw hard times in Germany, stimulating a large immigration to the United States. Groups of these immigrants settled in small pockets in Illinois, Missouri, Iowa, and Minnesota. Waterloo became one of those pockets, possibly because the first few settlers found the land similar to what they left behind in Germany. As the immigration continued, more settlers congregated out of kinship, forming a German enclave. These immigrants worked for the landholders for property ownership as well as for monetary pay. And they were successful! By the early 1900s, a great deal of the land was owned by people of German descent. They brought with them the ethnic characteristics of being hard working, enterprising, religious, and frugal.

In the early 1800s, there were three small communities which had been established along the Kaskaskia Trail about twenty miles south of the Cahokia Mounds. The southernmost town was named Bellefontaine. At the northern end of the settlement there was a small community called Peterstown. Less recognized, but frequently referred to by my grandmother's generation, was a separate settlement, Georgetown, that was located west of Peterstown along what is now Moore Street. These three communities coalesced into Waterloo, which became the county seat in 1825, and was officially chartered as a town in 1849.[1,3]

The area is rich in historical events, places and people. It was visited by General George Rogers Clark in 1778, was used as a jumping off place for the Lewis and Clark expedition in 1804, and was the site of the great chieftain Pontiac's assassination. Inhabited, influenced, or controlled by the Native Americans, Spanish, French, British, U.S. colonists, and German immigrants of the 1840s, the land around the major waterways holds a rich cultural heritage. And *my*

Meet My Waterloo   *Origins of the Town*

Waterloo sat in the middle of this storied and cultural stew as it grew from frontier watering hole for those few early adventurers to the full fledged town of over two thousand residents during my youth. For me, American history seemed at times to be a very local subject!

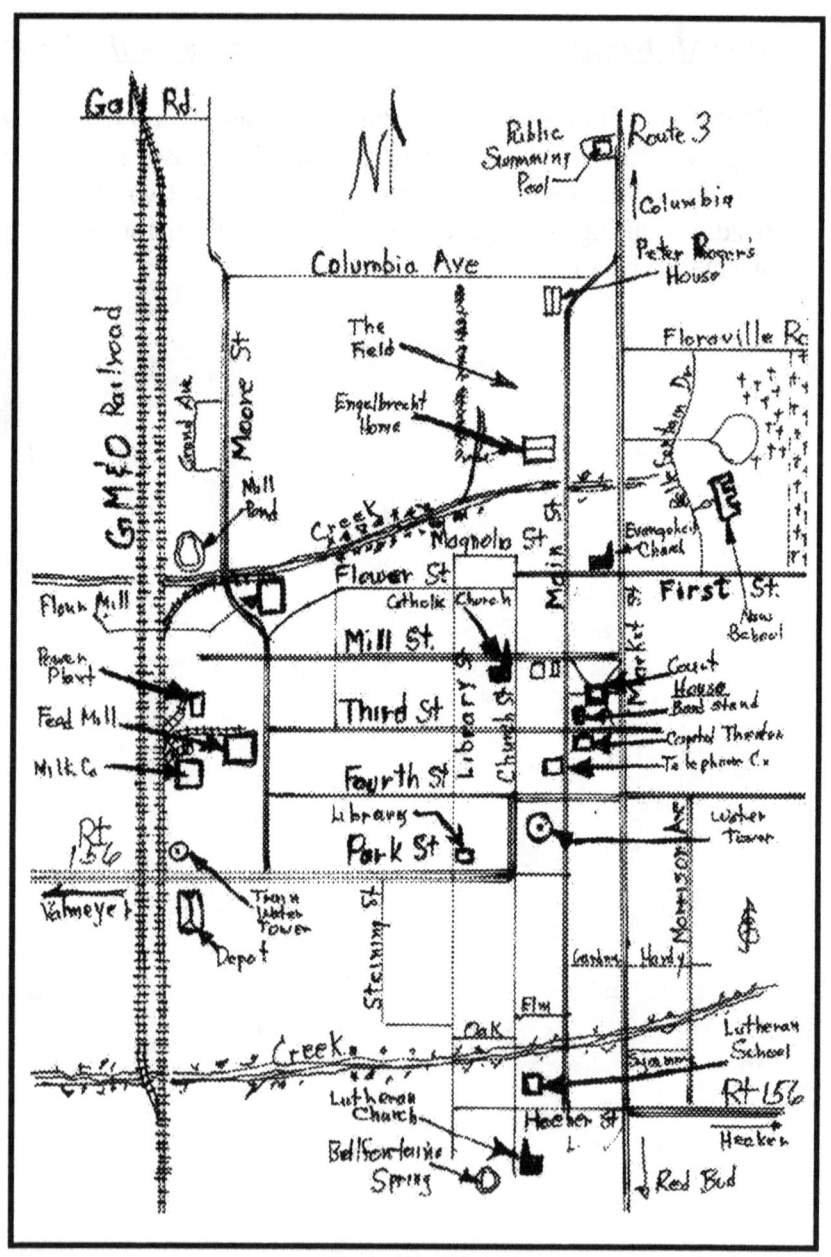

Waterloo Map

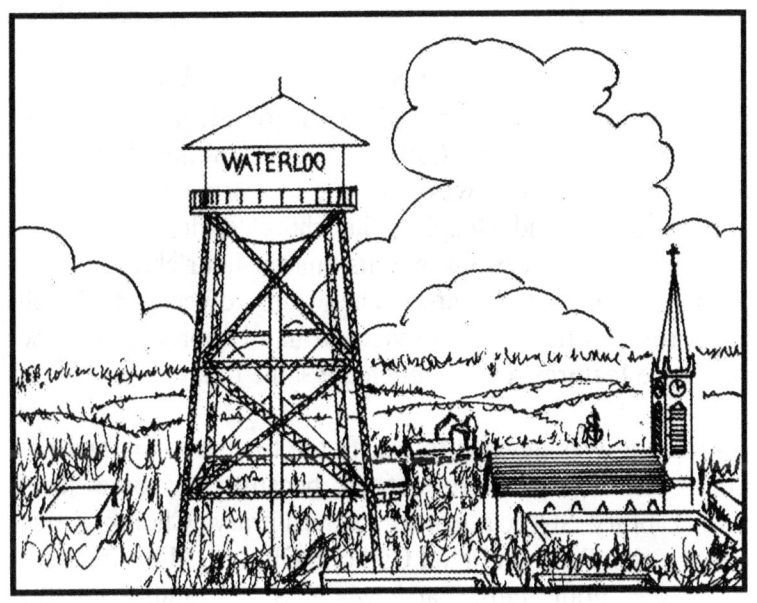

Waterloo Skyline

Chapter 2   My Town

Waterloo is situated on the edge of two geographic regions -- the great Ohio Valley Plains to the east and the Ozarks to the southwest. The Plains are characterized by level ground interspersed with remnants of forests which follow the courses of creeks and rivers. But the hilly country of the Ozarks also has its influence. As a result, the area is somewhat hilly with patches of level farmland and forest intermingled. The rolling hills provide excellent drainage for farming, and myriad creeks support the runoff of the summer's rain towards the Mississippi River.

The business portion of the town was located on the crest of a modest hill, with the county courthouse occupying the central square at the hill's apex. The land sloped downward towards creeks to the north and south of "downtown." A water tower was located on this high ground to ensure adequate pressure throughout the town. The Catholic Church, although slightly downhill from the crest, was none-the-less prominent because of its tall belfry and steeple. The church's clock could be viewed from four directions, and its quarter-hour chimes could be heard throughout the area. The water tower and church steeple provided the signature view from all approaches to the town. These features remain much the same today.

Street naming was devised to satisfy the townspeople, and not visitors. The names were chosen because of some local feature; Library Street ran next to the library, Church Street passed the Sts. Peter and Paul Catholic Church, Mill Street led towards the flour mills, and Main Street addressed the commercial establishments. Some naming was used to honor prominent citizens, thus Moore Street, Morrison Avenue, Hoener Street, and Steining Street came into existence. Only for a few blocks near the center of town does street naming surrender to a naming convention. The streets are "numbered," but even here Mill Street replaces Second Street. With this hodgepodge of conventions, giving directions to a stranger was difficult until you learned the art. The most useful technique in giving directions was to "point and steer." "Go to the top of the hill and turn right at the bank, then go two doors down on your right" was easier than explaining how to first find the streets, and then the desired location.

Route 3 traversed Waterloo in the north-south direction. While within the boundaries of the town, it was called Market Street. Route 3 provided the main connection to Columbia to the north and Red Bud to the south. Route 156 zigzaged its way through town and provided the main connection between Valmeyer to the west and Hecker to the east. Main Street,

Meet My Waterloo *My Town*

where my home was located, paralleled Market Street for most of the town. Typical of small farming communities, our town boundaries did not conform to well defined "edges" between urban features and rural farmland. Therefore, even though my home was well within the town boundaries, there was a field in back of my house which separated old Peterstown from old Georgetown. This field was regularly farmed, giving me a first hand education in agricultural practices, and I didn't even have to leave my yard!

The western edge of our community was bounded by the Gulf, Mobile, and Ohio (GM&O) railroad tracks. Between these tracks and Moore Street you would find the depot, Koenigsmark's Mill, the power plant, Horn's Mill, and the Waterloo Milk Company, representing our "heavy industries."

Most of the streets in the town were tree lined. The shaded sidewalks were a pleasant place to walk, especially on a hot summer day. But *I* didn't walk. The town was great for me because its topology provided hills, creeks, and fields that were all within easy running or biking distance. One could pump a bike uphill, and then "free-hand" down. The creeks, with their tree lined banks, were ideal for the game of Hide-and-Seek or the more sophisticated version for us savvy kids, Cops-and-Robbers. The nearby fields provided ample opportunity to race upwind to launch a kite. Whoever heard of walking!

Since one could reach the most distant boundary of Waterloo in about twenty minutes, the whole town became a play yard for my friends and me. And our parents did not worry about our safety; having a yard that size was acceptable. The town was safe because we children were known by many of the townspeople, who then became remote "eyes and ears" for our parents. On many an occasion, my mischief beat me home.

WPA Church Street Culvert Project

Chapter 3   My Time

Waterloo became "mine" in the time span encompassing the Great Depression through World War II. For adults, these were extremely hard times, but it was not the same for children of the era. Our generation of children was shielded from the serious effects of the times by our parents, our stable extended family, and our natural ability to play.

During the late 1920s, my father, who worked in St. Louis and lived in Waterloo, was courting my mother, a resident of nearby Chester. Courtship became difficult when my bookkeeper father was "offered" a transfer to Chicago by his accounting firm. Because work was hard to acquire during those Depression years, he accepted the transfer. The new difficulty of courtship was solved when my parents eloped in

Meet My Waterloo   *My Time*

October 1930 and moved into a furnished apartment on Chicago's North Side. I was born at the end of August in 1931. During the next year, the presidential election brought about a change of power between political parties and that made a significant difference in who had jobs and who did not. We became "have nots," and as have nots, my parents piled everything they owned into our car and moved to St. Louis, where my father again found work. Our living in St. Louis brought great joy to my grandparents because now we were close enough to visit often. Too soon, in 1935 my paternal grandfather died, leaving my grandmother to live alone in the town of Waterloo. Additionally, the Depression continued taking its toll, and my father was once again out of a job. Consequently, our family moved in with my grandmother in Waterloo in 1935. Her house became my home from that time through my high school graduation.

The Depression was difficult for adults, but not for most children. We always had food on the table, my clothes were always clean (or at least started that way), and Dad worked at whatever employment there was to make sure that we managed. Most families lived under these same Depression circumstances, and that included us kids.

I had almost no material possessions including toys, but neither did most of the other kids, so none of us felt deprived. This absence of "things" turned out to be a good lesson in disguise. We learned to play games that required little or no additional equipment. Tag, Hide-and-Seek, and Keep-Away were all games that one could play with nothing but enthusiasm. The investment in equipment for Kick-the-Can was manageable! For entertainment, we had radio, band concerts, and parades, all of which were free. Everything about the yard became a potential play object. And we had friends.

These blessings and conditions were reflected in a song entitled "Playmate,"[4] popular in the late Depression, and recalled here to the best of my recollection:

> *Playmate,*
> *Come out and play with me,*
> *And bring your (boys: "soldiers;" girls: "dollies") three,*
> *Climb up my apple tree,*
> *Hide in my rain barrel,*
> *Slide down my cellar door,*
> *And we'll be jolly friends,*
> *Forevermore.*

While the song acknowledges some personal possessions, the majority of the play objects are "household" items. Even today, when I see a cellar door, I recall this little song so reminiscent of those times.

In the depths of the Depression, government sponsored work became necessary for the country's well being. The Civilian Conservation Corps (CCC) and Work Projects Administration (WPA) were two programs that resulted from government action. My father worked for the CCC, which engaged in planting forests, cleaning creeks, and other manual workforce tasks. The WPA constructed bridges and drains, dredged rivers, built schools, and helped refurbish streets, accomplishing many of these projects through contractors. My bookkeeper father found the manual labor of the CCC very difficult, and all for the poor pay of thirty dollars a month. Conditions became even worse when he was injured on the job and had to spend several months in a military hospital at Jefferson Barracks, Missouri.

During this time, our insufficient income was augmented by what meager savings we and my grandmother had put aside earlier. Those funds were rapidly dwindling towards depletion when my father was able to find work again in St. Louis in his profession, and therefore, in the late 1930s we managed to recover financially. Now he would wear a suit and tie to work every day and his demeanor revealed his pride that he could once again be gainfully employed in the field of his choosing.

We kept abreast of world news through the newspaper and radio. The fact that a different kind of tumultuous world was developing in Europe and Asia was evident and was commonly discussed at the dinner table. I remember my uncle Wilbur visiting one Sunday and my father and uncle discussing the frightening prospects of another World War. I recall hearing for the first time some unfamiliar names and events: the Spanish Civil War, Franco, Ethiopia, Mussolini, Haile Selassie, Chamberlain, Churchill and, of course, Hitler, all relating to the news being reported from Europe. And while much attention was being given to the situation in Europe, my uncle was the one who said he really feared a war in Asia because of the conflict between Japan and China. He was scoffed at for that opinion, but how right he was!

I was playing table tennis at a friend's house on Sunday afternoon, December 7, 1941. We were in the basement engaged in a vigorous game. The family had the radio on upstairs. Suddenly, we heard a shout and we quickly raced up to see what was wrong. I remember listening to the newscasts describing the events of Pearl Harbor. And so, that day ushered in a new era that affected growing up in Waterloo, one that transitioned from our having had few material possessions due to the Depression, to now having few possessions due to rationing for World War II. It also changed the town from a male dominated environment to one in which women played an extremely important role in the conduct of business -- a role they would never relinquish.

Rationing and price controls were required during World War II. Rationing was invoked because much of the production of the country had to go to the war effort. Furthermore, it was necessary to restrain spending which could create inflation and encourage black markets. Price controls were therefore placed into force to manage the effect of the resulting unnatural supply and demand dynamics. Workers were needed for military production, young men were required for the armed services, and business continued to require employees, all of which made jobs and money available. Rationing kept the spending down, so citizens began to accumulate savings. Therefore, war bonds and stamps were introduced to help finance the war effort, and offer a way to patriotically invest that money.

Many of the businesses in the town were run either by a man who started his business or one who took over the business from parents. As the Selective Service drafted more and more men for service, wives took over for their husbands. Additionally, many of the women who had been at-home mothers while their children were growing up, now worked in the war effort. Quitting time at many of the local places of work saw an equal number of men and women exiting -- the men older than the age being drafted, the women, young wives of husbands now in the service. The absence of so many of the young men from the town even created work opportunities for some of the children in the upper grade school levels, and I was fortunate enough to have one of those jobs during the war. (But more about that later!)

The World War II time frame was a period of intense citizen loyalty for all the people in the town. Patriotism imitated religion, and rivaled it in devotion and expression. How strange it must have been to people from other communities to see the loyalty of these German descendants speaking angrily about "that awful Hitler" and "*those* Germans" while the young men proudly and patriotically entered military service. This patriotism gave little thought to the fact that the warring opponents could well be relatives; but later, as losses on both sides mounted, the thought became inescapable. Towards the end of the war, German POWs were brought to the United States. To minimize the incentive for escape, the prison camps were located far into the interior of the country. One such POW camp was within the town of Waterloo, fairly near my house. It was a minimally guarded facility with a barbed wire fence around the perimeter, and tents set up in the enclosure to shelter the prisoners. At first, I was afraid to have these dangerous enemies so close to my home, but, bowing to curiosity, my friends and I would venture as close as we dared to see what the enemy was like. For these prisoner soldiers, tired from years of fighting, there was no desire to escape, or make trouble, and they would just wave when they saw us gawking. I remember seeing our townspeople going to the camp on Sunday afternoons, carrying trays of food for the POWs in exchange for the opportunity to talk with them regarding conditions and relatives in Germany. I could not help but think what a strange world we live in. War was bad on both sides.

Part II
The Heartbeat of the Town

Chapter 4 The Tradesmen

Chapter 5 The Word Gets Around

Chapter 6 Entertainment

Tradesmen at the "Roger's Seminary" Apartments

Chapter 4   The Tradesmen

Fast food chains. One-hour photo processing. Drive-in cleaners. Drive-through banking. Today, we seem to have grown dependent on the service industries and some people are critical of our need to get what we want when we want it. In reality, the concept of service has been around a long time, but its manifestation has changed. When I was a boy, we did not drive to the service, it came to us! If you lived in my town, doorstep delivery was the norm. The iceman delivered directly to the icebox located at your home. The milkman delivered to your front doorstep. The bakery van delivered fresh goods on a daily basis. The mailman walked through yards delivering the mail to each house. The produce men, (usually local farmers), brought fresh goods from the farm. Groceries could be ordered and were delivered on certain days of the week.

Meet My Waterloo   *The Tradesmen*

And even the doctor would make house calls. Now that's service!

The Iceman
The iceman made daily rounds of the town using his pickup truck loaded with blocks of ice purchased from the milk company. The milk company was a source for ice for the entire town as well as for its own refrigeration needs. Several competing merchants participated in the deliveries.

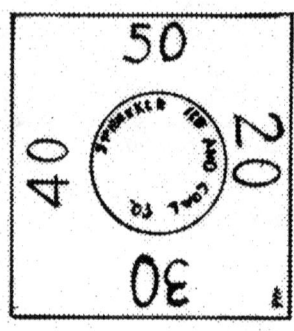

Communication between the household and the iceman was through the use of a square, colored card. On each side of the card there were four different numbers, each indicating the number of pounds of ice desired. The numbers were placed on the card in such a manner that the top of each number was always at one of the edges of the card. Therefore when the card was placed in your window, only one number would be correctly oriented. That number indicated the amount of ice you needed that day. Different colored cards were used for the different merchants.

Upon seeing your order, the ice truck driver would stop at your home. He would skillfully chip off an amount of ice estimated to fill the order. This block was subsequently weighed to ensure that the amount being delivered was reasonably close to your request, and then it was carried into the home. First, the ice that remained in the icebox was removed, then the new block was inserted, and last, the old

Meet My Waterloo   The Tradesmen

block was chipped to fill the leftover space. All this service came with the ice delivery.

On a hot summer day, it was a delight for the children to see the ice truck. As the blocks were chipped to fill the custom orders shown in the window, small pieces of ice would flake off from the block and remain on the truck bed. As soon as the iceman disappeared into a home for his delivery, we would rush to the truck to get these refreshing pieces. Even when no chipping was required, there always was some spare ice available on the truck bed. The iceman must have been a kid himself once!

There were certain merchants engaged in multiple businesses to service the town. As examples, the iceman also dealt in coal; the furniture dealer was also the undertaker. The ice business would flourish in the late spring, summer, and early fall, but demand for ice dropped severely during the winter. And while it seemed strange to me, at the time, for the vendor for refrigeration to engage also in the delivery of coal for heat, this combination made sense, giving the merchant steady revenue throughout the year. The furniture man's complementary business was not such an obvious match until you realized that both "services" originally required a cabinet maker. My grandmother found grim humor in this arrangement, commenting, "He gets you coming and he gets you going!"

The Milkman
Dairy product deliveries were made to your doorstep. The milkman's route was covered with a horse-drawn cart, and the route was so regular that he did not need to guide his horse -- the horse knew each and every stop. When he was ready to move to the next location, the milkman would make a clicking

sound with his tongue and the horse would amble to the next stop while the milkman prepared his next delivery.

Remember, communication with the iceman was made through the colored card, but the technique for the milkman was much simpler. You placed the appropriate number of empty bottles on your porch or doorstep to indicate order quantity. However, you did include a note with detailed instructions, as well, with requests for other products. Deliveries to each household were fairly predictable, therefore the milkman would put the most probable order in his wire basket and go to your doorstep. He would take the selections from his basket, place them on the doorstep, retrieve the empty bottles, and go on to the next neighbor.

The array of products available from the milkman included regular milk, homogenized milk, smooth and large curd cottage cheese, buttermilk, and butter. We, as a household, always ordered the regular milk. The cream on this product would rise to the top, and my grandmother would pour off the cream for use in cooking and coffee. The remaining fresh milk was for ordinary household use. We frequently purchased the smooth cottage cheese, for it had a wonderful flavor unique (and evidently secret) to that company. Not only was it a special treat for us, but it was popular throughout the town. I have never been able to find another vendor that could duplicate that specialty.

The milkman would come at a fairly regular time, and therefore each household would retrieve the milk from the porch soon after delivery. Occasionally the household routine would be interrupted for one reason or another, and on an especially cold winter day, the milk would freeze.

Meet My Waterloo *The Tradesmen*

Milk, composed mostly of water, would expand as it froze, and a large cylinder of frozen cream and milk would rise out of the bottle with the cap sitting jauntily atop the frozen mass. How angry my grandmother would be that she could let this happen and now would have to be so careful bringing this frozen blob into the house!

<u>The Bakery Van</u>
While there were several bakeries in the town, one specific entrepreneur brought bakery products directly to your home. Gene Mechler modified his four-door automobile so that the back seat and trunk space had many tiers of shelves. Early in the morning, freshly baked goods were loaded into his mobile store, and he would make the rounds of the town. His was one delivery that you could always anticipate coming. The only practical way to vend his goods was to have you come to the van to see the collection. Whenever he got to a customer's home, therefore, he would blow the horn as his invitation. Since you could hear his horn several customers away, you could begin anticipating your order.

One of the primary products purchased through this service was freshly baked bread. It was characteristic of every household to serve a large stack of white bread with each meal. I suspect that the bread was a "filler," but in any case it was delicious. As a treat, however, my grandmother would occasionally purchase cream puffs, flaky rolls filled with a lemon cream custard. These would be served as a surprise at the breakfast table. When guests were expected, stolen and coffee cake would be selected, but they could not be touched until the guests were served.

The Farmers
Waterloo was surrounded by farms. Most of these farms had large acreage in wheat, corn, oats and other grain products. However, they also had substantial plots dedicated to growing produce. This produce would not only help feed the farm families, but sufficient quantities were grown that it could also be sold to the nearby communities. It was fairly typical in the summertime to see a horse-drawn "hay wagon" filled with produce slowly moving its way down the street. One or more of the farmer's children would run ahead of the wagon and knock on doors or ring doorbells to attract the attention of the homeowners and announce that produce was available at the wagon. These products were always fresh, and would be purchased by my grandmother primarily for the purpose of canning or storing for use during the winter. For such products as potatoes, apples, and pears, storage would be accomplished by simply placing them in the "fruit cellar." Other items like beans, cherries, peas, and tomatoes would be canned. Seasonal food stuffs including corn, beets, watermelon and cantaloupe, would also be purchased for daily consumption.

The Doctor
House calls! How I dreaded the doctor's house call. It meant you were really sick or hurt. And worst of all, if you were sick, how you dreaded the contagious diseases. If one contracted the measles, mumps, chickenpox, or other similar diseases, it was required that a huge sign be placed on your home warning others of the potential contagion. On the first outward sign that one was seriously ill, the doctor would be notified, and he would schedule a visit to your home. Dr. Werth was probably one of the more friendly people you could have visit you, but knowing the implication of his visit made it hard for me to be friendly back. He would check with your parents, probe your body, and question you about your

symptoms all to determine your specific ailment. Medication, if required, would be prescribed, and invariably, you were to be kept calm and quiet in a dark room. The doctor would then leave and report the illness to some county agency (and I still don't know what the agency might be). Within a day, a large "QUARANTINE" notice, officially signed, would be delivered defining the nature of the illness, the date when it was first noted, and the date when the quarantine would be over. This notice had to be posted in a highly visible place at the most frequently used door to your home so that tradesmen and visitors would be aware of the illness, and could avoid contracting or spreading the sickness.

The Neighborhood Stores
The majority of the town businesses were located "downtown," and because everyone walked to their destination during the Depression and war, each section of the town had its own local "mom and pop" grocery store that flourished because it could shorten your walk and save time. Boehne's was located in the southern part of town near the library, Vogt's and Sendelbeck's on the west side near the mills, Reitz's, on the east side, and Kuhn's, on the north side of town near my home, to name a few. These local stores were used for "incidental" shopping, that is, the things you forgot at the downtown stores, or ran out of in the middle of some cooking chore.

Kuhn's store was located about a block from my home, and I ran many an errand there for my grandmother. Mr. Kuhn was the epitome of our ethnic culture. He was tall, large featured, slightly stooped with age, and he shuffled as he walked about the store. He sported a large gray handlebar mustache, and had curly waxed hair, rosy cheeks, and friendly eyes. His voice was soft and gentle, and his eyes twinkled with delight to see you. Arm bands tugged on his sleeves to keep his cuffs above his wrists, and a sleeveless vest captured his tie, both restraints being necessary when he bent over to scoop produce from barrels. His clothes were protected by a bibbed apron which was usually quite smudged by the end of the day.

His store was a long narrow structure that adjoined his residence. One of the small walls formed the front of the store and had the only two windows that let in some light. The store was otherwise quite dark and lights hanging from the ceiling were usually required even on the brightest of summer days. The high ceiling was covered in metallic mosaic, and the floor was oiled wood.

The long wall on the right as you entered the store was lined with shelving. Glass jars occupied some of the space and contained foods such as dried beans, nuts, and spices. Crocks held a variety of brines used for storing pickles, beets, sauerkraut, and fruit. Wooden boxes acting as drawers held the fresh produce usually bought from the local farmers. Barrels replaced some of the lower shelving to provide storage space for bulkier or higher volume products such as flour and potatoes. Towards the rear, shelves stored household accessories such as shelf lining paper, dish towels, oilcloth, can openers, and wooden spoons. In front of most of the shelving there was a long counter used to aid in the packaging of the foodstuffs for your order, or as a cutting board for your custom length product.

The long wall to the left of the structure was used for a variety of storage needs. The tobacco dispensary was located near the front of the store. These shelves contained the cartons of cigarettes, plugs of chewing tobacco, tins and sacks of pipe tobacco, and brightly decorated boxes of cigars. These

Meet My Waterloo *The Tradesmen*

products were stored behind large glass cabinet doors, and one would almost be overcome with the sweet fragrance of tobacco when those doors were opened and they released their concentrated scents.

Just beyond the door to Mr. Kuhn's private quarters, there was additional shelving, primarily dedicated to commercial canned goods, cereals, and baking supplies. These shelves extended about halfway along the length of the wall. The remaining wall space had a number of horizontal boards mounted to it, each board having numerous hooks. This space was used to store the meat for the "butcher" department. Dried beef, sausages of every description, cured hams, and other smoked and dried meats were hung from these hooks. A butcher block counter stood in front of this meat rack. Above the butcher block there was a horizontal wooden bar also equipped with hooks. This bar hung from the ceiling, and held the saws, cleavers, and knives needed for meat carving.

Counter space also lined the long left wall. The counter closest to the front of the store and directly in front of the tobacco cabinet was the candy counter. The candy was located behind a long curved glass viewing panel with cabinet doors in the rear. Because the counter was too high for the very young, wooden soda cases turned upside down were used as a step along the front. Behind the glass, the candy was displayed in their cardboard containers, one box neatly stacked against the next. Gum drops, red licorice sticks, black licorice sticks, red hots, colored jelly beans, black jelly beans, caramel balls, malt drops, sugared orange slices, and chocolate covered raisins teased your taste buds. And each box showed you the price, from the economical ten-for-a-penny to the expensive one-for-a-penny. Some candies, such as "dots," came attached to a strip of paper, and this you bought by the foot. There were a few candy bars, but these bars, at a nickel each, made it seem more practical to go after the quantity available through the purchase of the "penny stock." The glass case was covered with nose prints. It was a fact well known by all of the local kids that you could stare a piece of candy out of the case by just fixing your gaze on it. It would not take long before Mr. Kuhn would open the case, and as if reading your mind, select the exact piece of your desired confection, asking, "Would you like to have a piece of candy?" It worked almost every time, or at least the first time you visited the store that day.

The next counter supported the baked goods cabinet. This cabinet was a four sided glass enclosure holding fresh pastries and bread. Along side of this case was a roll of "butcher paper" for wrapping your purchases.

Many of the homes during this era used kerosene stoves for cooking, especially in the summer time when it was too hot to use the coal stove. Additionally, small upright kerosene heaters were sometimes used in the spring and fall to warm a room early in the morning. Mr. Kuhn stored kerosene in a small shed located on the sidewalk in front of his store. This shed had the appearance of a "wishing well" with enclosed sides. The bottom of the building housed the kerosene storage tank, and the top, when opened, gave access to the metered pump used for dispensing the liquid to your container.

While these neighborhood stores did not regularly provide delivery service, Mr. Kuhn's store had a special feature. He employed a woman by the name of Emma Stoeckel to help tend the store. Emma lived about twice as far from the store on Main Street as we did. At night, when she would walk home, she would deliver to any house along her route as long as the request was not heavy. We enjoyed a special privilege because my grandmother and Mrs. Stoeckel were the best of friends, and when she stopped by our house, the two ladies would converse in their beloved "Low Deutsche," a colloquial German dialect spoken almost exclusively by their generation in the early 1900s. With the passage of time, fewer and fewer people used it, giving way to the influence of English, the only language now taught in the schools.

Downtown
The "downtown" portion of Waterloo was the center for commerce. But for a kid, it was just a description of places you visited, and the names of businesses were as useful as street signs. Four large grocery stores were concentrated on one block of Mill street. Rau's, Schmitt's, and Kroger's shared one side of the street, and Henke's stood alone on the other side. Three banks commanded Main Street with the Commercial State, First National, and State Bank all in one block across from the court house. Main Street also housed the Schulmeister Bakery, Harrisonville Telephone Company, and Eilbracht's and Hamacher's pharmacies, Back's and Mueller's dry goods stores, Rexroth's and Roever's restaurants (although Rex's was officially a confectionery), Quernheim's and Wagner's funeral homes and furniture stores, the Southern and City hotels, Wallhaus's hardware store, and the Capitol Theatre. Schoeneberg's Shoe Repair and Glessner's Shoe Repair split their allegiances between Mill Street and Main Street respectively. Three newspapers vied for the county business, and these were the *Waterloo Times*, the *Waterloo Republican*, and the *Monroe County Clarion*. Other businesses included a meat market, several automobile dealerships, a farm implement dealership, a tinsmith, a gas distributor, and several barber shops.

Industry

Large employers of the town included the two mills, the milk company, and later, a clothing factory. The mills and milk company needed railroad access and therefore they were located on Moore Street. Both mills processed grain, but for two different segments of the industry. One ground flour for human consumption, and the other processed feed for livestock. One mill was known as Koenigsmark's Flour Mill and it distributed a private brand of flour named "Silverfox." This mill had the capacity to store large quantities of wheat, and could produce the flour throughout the year. The other mill was known as Horn's Feed Mill. Both had vigorous activity in the summer when the farmers brought their grain for processing.

Many of the farms had herds of cattle raised for meat and milk production. The Waterloo Milk Company processed milk from the surrounding farms and distributed the resulting dairy products locally through their own delivery service and through the stores. In order to preserve these products, the company engaged in the production of vast amounts of ice that was also sold to the community through the icemen. The company had several aliases, one of which was the "Creamery," so named because of its products. I grew up under the false impression that another nickname, the "Condensery," was assigned because of its high cooling tower (steam condenser) when, in fact, that name originated because of earlier condensed milk production.

At one time, many of the towns in this part of the country had an industry known as the knitting mills, and these were large employers of women. However, by the early 1930s, most of these mills had disappeared, and women had little opportunity for employment. With the outbreak of World War II, a lingerie factory in nearby Millstadt began to also produce parachutes, and needed more workers. Many of the women of Waterloo, including my mother, formed a carpool and began to work at the factory. Shortly after that opening, a company called Rice-Stix started a garment factory in Waterloo in an abandoned school building. The carpool group rapidly changed jobs to this factory in order to reduce the driving and the hardship imposed by gas rationing.

German genes require beer, and therefore there were twelve taverns in the town, and all of them prospered. There probably would have been more if the quantity had not been restrained by city ordinance. As it was, there were more taverns than grocery stores or churches. When you count the multiple bartenders required for the steady business enjoyed by the taverns, you realize that this "industry" was among the largest employers.

The Tradesmen and Me
With so many businesses, the town was fairly self-sufficient in its ability to provide almost any service necessary for its residents. Additionally, these businesses offered a significant local employment base. Being the Monroe County Seat made Waterloo itself the hub of the county. Most of the businesses were known to all of us in town, either because we dealt directly with them or knew the people that worked there.

These businesses were part of my childhood; I routinely visited them on my assigned errands. Some however, had special significance. Kuhn's neighborhood store almost seemed to be an extension of my home because I was sent there so often (and don't forget the candy). Rau's Grocery Store became a place of my employment, and it was as Coralyn Rau's grocery boy that I became acquainted with so

Meet My Waterloo   The Tradesmen

many of the townspeople (and they, me). Schoeneberg's Shoe Repair was owned by "Chappie" Schoeneberg, my grandmother's brother, who took over the shoe repair business from my great grandfather. Chappie ate dinner and supper (*you* call them "lunch" and "dinner") with us every day, and were it not for his irascible demeanor, he could easily have been a lovable member of the family.

Koenigsmark's Flour Mill holds a special place in my life even though I remember little of it. My paternal grandfather worked most of his life in the mill and was very proud of his job as a miller. My earliest recollection of him is his holding me in his arms and "showing me off" to his fellow workers. He took a glass "Mason" jar and held it in an opening in a chute delivering newly processed flour to show me what it looked like. We had few opportunities to really know each other since he died when I was three, so this recollection of the mill visit is especially precious.

The Rice-Stix garment factory work was very rewarding to my mother. She was overjoyed with the opportunity to work and have an income of her own. The group of women that worked together became lifelong friends, and it was a joy to see my mother extend her circle of acquaintances.

The Switchboard Operators

Chapter 5   The Word Gets Around

Recently, we changed from standard to daylight savings time, which required resetting eighteen time oriented devices including clocks, personal time pieces, and controls for appliances, electronics, and utilities. When I was young, we had only one clock in the house that was the primary time keeper and that clock agreed perfectly with those in other homes. Many of the residents did not have a radio for coordinating time, and therefore the town had numerous ways of communicating "Waterloo" time through the town siren, church bells, and factory whistles, and conveying information through the telephone operators. With this array of devices, the community was self-synchronized and informed.

Meet My Waterloo   *The Word Gets Around*

There were other sources of information for many of the residents including the daily newspapers and radio. Local and county newspapers kept people informed on a weekly basis. St. Louis newspapers provided daily insight about what was happening in the nearby big city and the rest of the world. They became a significant source of information during World War II. The radio's role in our lives was primarily one of entertainment. While there were some news broadcasts, they were short and reported only the most significant headlines. You listened to be entertained, and did not "wait up" for the news on the radio. Real time news was gleaned from the telephone.

The Telephone
The Harrisonville Telephone Company provided communication within our county. The technology used at that time is known by today's standard as "hoot and holler" because, within reason, the louder you talked the farther you could communicate. Each telephone company had its own local territory, and engineered its system to compensate for most of the unique line losses. However, unlike today's technology, there were no repeaters in the system to compensate for excessive or unusual line losses. Whatever energy left your microphone was all that the system had to work with. Compensating within your own system could usually be handled by talking a little louder. But long distance was another story. Long distance involved at least two territories, each of which could suffer these losses. I can remember screaming (hollering) into the telephone's microphone so that relatives in distant California could hear what we had to say from Waterloo.

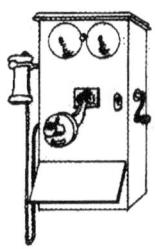 The telephone consisted of a large rectangular box about a foot wide, a foot deep and two feet long, usually mounted to the wall. The bells announcing the receipt of a call were mounted near the top of the front face of the telephone. Below the bells came the mouthpiece or microphone mounted on the end of a long arm which could be raised and lowered to match the height of the individual standing in front of the telephone. A small tilted "writing table" was located at the lower end of the front face. On the left side of the box was the ear piece (receiver), about the size of a tumbler and connected by a long cord. Finally, on the right side, there was the hand crank to supply a ringing signal to the operator. The arrangement of the telephone was directed to the predominantly right handed population with the left hand holding the ear piece, and the right hand engaged in the dexterous movements of crank turning and writing.

To initiate a call, one would remove the ear piece from the hook on the side of the telephone, and this action activated a switch that connected you to the central office. By turning the crank, an electrical signal was created that caused an indicator at the central office switchboard to be released (hence the name "drop"). In front of the operator, there were two rows of electrical connectors. The operator would take a rear connector and plug it into the receptacle just below your "drop" on the board while resetting the drop. By operating a switch associated with the chords, the operator could talk with you ("Number, please?") and you orally conveyed the telephone number of the party wanted. (In a small town like mine, a name was just as good since the operators had memorized the telephone book.) The operator would then return the switch to the neutral position, take the second connector associated with that call and plug it into the desired telephone number position on the board. The switch would then be operated in the opposite direction, and the operator would ring the number of the desired party. When the call was answered, the operator would again return the switch to the neutral position and the two parties were connected. When the conversation was through, the originating party would again ring the telephone by turning the crank. This was known as the "ring off." Again the drop at the operator's switchboard would change, signifying to the operator that the call was through and the cords could be unplugged.

Use of the telephone became personal between you and the operator. You knew all the operators, and they knew you, and your number. The conversation could be as simple as "703 please" or, if you forgot the number, "Rosemary, connect me to Alma at Deppy's, please." Now here is where communication really took place. Her (and it was always a woman) reply might be, "This is Alma's day off, would you like to talk to Deppy or shall I call Alma at her house?" This telephone company knew your schedule, and could track you down!

I did not use the telephone much as a child. First of all, the mouthpiece was slightly too high for me and I had to stand on tiptoes to reach it. Furthermore, most of the things we kids wanted to talk about were much better discussed in private, out of our parents' earshot. Finally, the telephone was really not my friend. While I had free reign of the town and could have my adventures wherever I wanted, invariably when I got into mischief, news of the deed reached home long before I did. This was one of the children's hazards in a small town -- everyone knew you.

The Siren

Synchronization of the community's time was assigned to the fire siren. The siren was mounted to a cross member of the water tower since the tower was the town's highest public structure and was centrally located.

The primary purpose of the siren was to summon the volunteer fire department. The town was divided into four wards, and the siren would be blown the number of times corresponding to the ward in which the fire was located. This enabled the volunteer firemen to get a start in the right direction. The exact location of the fire was known by the crew on duty at the firehouse, and the wailing of their fire trucks would guide the volunteers directly to it.

The siren was also used to announce noon and 6:00 P.M. of each day. Almost everyone in business and at home had their midday meal (dinner) at exactly noon and ate their evening meal (supper) at exactly 6:00 P.M. When the whistle sounded signifying the call to dinner or supper, my grandmother would immediately start placing the food on the table knowing that diners would be assembled momentarily. At the noon siren alert, Chappie closed his shoe repair business and arrived at our house within minutes. I would leave school from the farthest part of town, hop on my bike, and also be home within minutes. Promptness was the key to hot food!

Another use for the siren was to announce a curfew. Curfew was instigated for two purposes. The first was to make sure that children younger than thirteen were off the street and at home by 9:00 P.M. -- my grandmother referred to it as the "kinder curfew." During the war, the second reason for curfew was to announce "Lights Out" during air raid drills.

The curfew for kids was a serious matter. To get in the maximum amount of play, one never started home until you heard the siren, and then, of course, it was too late. Since we used the alert as a timing signal rather than a restriction to public activity, we needed to be very discreet in our choice of a route home. We made judicious use of alleys to stay out of sight; however, I can not remember a single child being apprehended for breaking curfew. Even today, I wonder how much grace period we had.

I do remember one specific evening when I had been playing at my friend Roland's home, and his parents warned me about the impending curfew. I headed home, walking in an alley (a short cut) next to the water tower. Just that moment, the curfew was to be sounded. The start-up sound of the siren was a powerful rumble -- as frightening as any imaginary ghost could sound. The siren soon reached its full pitch and then I realized what was happening, but the damage from my fright had already been done. I raced home, continually looking over my shoulder to see if I was being followed.

The Mill Whistle
The Koenigsmark Mill also announced its starting and stopping times with the blowing of its steam whistle. Each person working there was expected to be at his position when the whistle blew in the morning and after dinner, and each person knew that he could leave this position when the whistle blew at noon and in the evening. While these signals were intended for plant schedules, the remainder of the town within earshot also used these signals as timing announcements.

The Church Clock

Sts. Peter and Paul Catholic Church was located near the center of town on high ground, giving additional stature to its high belfry and even higher steeple. On the upper reaches of the belfry there was a clock face for each of the cardinal directions. Below each clock face there was a shuttered opening so that the sound emanating from the clock's bells could escape from the belfry. During my childhood, the clock could be seen from almost every part of town and each face was sufficiently large that it was easy to read the time. Additionally, the clock's bell rang one peal at the quarter-hour, two at the half-hour, and three at the three-quarter's hour. The hour itself was counted out by the bell. This sound could be heard throughout town even if the clock face was obscured at your location. There was little tolerance for the excuse, "I didn't know what time it was."

Church Bells

Every church had a unique set of bells and style of ringing to announce events. The Evangelical Church, in addition to bells, had a set of musical chimes called a carillon. On Saturday evening, just after the siren's announcement that it was 6:00 P.M., all the churches would ring their bells to remind the residents that church service was being held the next day. Following this joyous ringing, hymns would be played on the Evangelical Church chimes. On Sunday morning, the first church to announce a service would be the Catholic Church signifying early mass. Later in the morning, one could hear several churches announcing the start of service and it was the festive sound of multiple churches ringing their bells of invitation.

During the week, the only church to announce church services was the Catholic Church, chiming its morning mass. This early morning pealing of the bells served as an alarm clock to many schoolchildren unless you were in the Catholic School. Those children had to attend that mass, in which case they had to get up much earlier. Thank goodness I was Lutheran!

Church bells also announced other events to the town. Many celebrations were scheduled in the afternoon and therefore most afternoon bells meant a wedding or baptism. Funerals could occur either in the morning or afternoon, but had their signature tolling of bells for the funeral service. That would be the moment that the town would say its last goodbye even from individuals not present at the service.

The Band Concert

Chapter 6   Entertainment

The people of Waterloo enjoy their companionship, and public events were welcomed as the opportunity to socialize. Band concerts, picnics, school plays, sports, and even the movies provided the venue for these gatherings.

The Band Concert
The Waterloo Municipal Band concert is given every Tuesday night during the summer. This ritual was a tradition when I was a boy and continues to this day. The presentation started at dusk, and lasted for about an hour. It was held at the town Bandstand, a small pavilion on the southwest corner of Court House Square. The square was an oak tree studded park surrounding the one hundred (plus) year old Monroe County Court House located at the center of the large block. The

Meet My Waterloo   *Entertainment*

Bandstand nestled in one of the square's corners, bordered by this dense oak grove on two sides, and Main Street and Third Street on the other two sides. The wooden structure's floor was about six feet off the ground. Its front side and stairway faced Main Street. A raised floor on three sides enabled the musicians on that level to see the band director over those seated on the main floor. The open platform was covered with a simple gabled roof to protect the musicians and their instruments during the frequent Midwest thunderstorms. Light fixtures, attached to the ceiling, flooded the stand with light during the concerts.

Makeshift "park benches" were assembled every Tuesday night in the grove, each bench consisting of two short sawbucks and a strong wooden plank placed between them. If you arrived early, you could stack several sawbucks as a fulcrum for a bench plank, creating a see-saw, but most of the time we were discouraged from disrupting the preparations. Since there were a limited number of these benches, each holding at most around eight people, it was advantageous to arrive early for the concert. The remainder of the ambulatory concert goers stood in back of those seated, or sat on their own lawn chairs to listen to the concert.

There was another important segment to the appreciative audience. These were the drive-in attendees who would listen from their vehicles, and show their appreciation by honking the horn as a substitute for applause. The town used diagonal parking in the downtown area, and the mobile concert goers would arrive as early as possible to get these choice "seats." In addition to the legitimate diagonal parking spaces, additional spaces were created using parallel parking directly in back of the diagonally parked cars. On the Third Street side of the "concert hall," the Bandstand is on your right, therefore, the

Meet My Waterloo   *Entertainment*

cars would be double parked on the proper side of the street to have a clear view of the event through the windshield. However, on the Main Street side, the Bandstand is on your left if you park to view the concert through the windshield, and consequently, the cars would be double parked facing the "wrong" direction for traffic flow. Strangers driving north on Main Street were often startled to see a line of cars facing them. Because the tradition was such an important event in the community's social life, the police ignored the obvious traffic violations, and instead, enjoyed the evening themselves.

During the Depression, the band concert was a wonderful free gift given by the band to the townspeople and it was greatly appreciated in a money starved era. The band was composed of community musicians whose time was donated. They loved their music, and enjoyed the opportunity to share their talent with the community. Many of the "regulars" were local businessmen and town leaders, and their numbers were augmented by high school students or recent graduates. These younger members would usually play with the band for a few years, then be enlisted by other priorities. But there was never any question about each member's dedication. Even in the off-season, on a cold winter's night, you could hear the band practicing the music they were to play the next summer. The sounds would emanate from the court room. This location was one of the few places with the combination of having enough seating space for the practice session and being free of charge. On those cold, crisp nights, it was a joy to stand outside for a few minutes (and that is all the time you could tolerate in an Illinois winter) to listen to the music being rehearsed, and you could speculate if you would remember the specific selection and occasion when it was played again at the summer concert.

Several members of the band are indelibly etched in my mind. One is Bryant Voris, a local newspaper publisher who was the band's "father figure." He not only directed the band, but he was instrumental in the continuing process of recruiting the membership to participate in this labor of love, and he selected the music to be played. His firm leadership with the baton was an inspiration in my young exposure to band music. My mother enjoyed relating the story of my standing on the running board of our 1932 Plymouth waving a stick as I proudly mimicked his conducting.

Jacob Bersche, a jewelry store owner, was the oldest member of the band. He was a short man, slightly stooped, with gray hair. His instrument was the piccolo, and *Stars and Stripes Forever*, his shining moment. The band concluded each evening's performance with the playing of that rousing, patriotic work. The march, like most marches, is played loudly and with vigor; however, there is one solo passage during the march that belongs solely to the piccolo. And that passage was Jacob's! The piccolo, under normal circumstances, does not create loud music, and played by Jacob, it created even less. But everyone knew that it was Jacob's solo, and all gossiping, noise making, and other activity ceased in order to hear his soft but precise rendition. The end of the music would elicit a rousing cheer and automobile horn salute in appreciation of the stirring performance.

Picnics
At the end of each school year, the district would hold a "School Picnic." Some years, the event was held at Pautler Park, a grove of trees near the railroad station. That site was particularity attractive to me since one corner of the park was the site for the train's water tower, and one could get a close view of the steam engines as they took on water. The picnic

| *Meet My Waterloo* | *Entertainment* |

was for the benefit of the children, with a Ferris Wheel being the center attraction. Games were held during the afternoon. They included the Sack Race (both feet in one sack), the Three Legged Race (one of your legs and one of your partner's in one sack), Dash (by age), and Tug-of-War. Park benches made of sawbucks with a board across them were soon confiscated for see-saws. The dance pavilion became a huge sliding board when the dance floor was dusted with the talcum that permitted dancers to "glide." Flavored ice cones, cotton candy and soda pop were the foods of the day, some of which could be purchased with free tickets donated by local merchants. In later years, the picnic was moved to the public school grounds, and it lost some of its charm, as well as shade, but it was still the end of the school year, and the beginning of SUMMER VACATION.

In August, Waterloo held its Homecoming Picnic, and this event was very popular with local and former residents. Town natives who had moved would return for this event to meet with friends and relatives. The festivities began Friday night on Main Street, directly in front of the courthouse. Attractions such as the Ferris Wheel and Tilt-O-Whirl were the draw for the younger generation. Both sides of the street were lined with booths, including vending stands for fish, hamburgers, Polish sausage, hot dogs, beer, soda, ice cream, and cotton candy. Additionally, there were four taverns along Main Street. Gambling booths supplied by the concessionaire included the Wheel-of-Fortune, Dime Toss, Bottle Ball, Balloon Darts, and the Shooting Gallery, all of which I can guarantee made much profit. The largest attraction was the bingo game, and you could hear the drone from the public address system over the entire town: "'I' five...that's five under 'I'...'O' sixty...that's sixty under 'O'..." and so on throughout the entire picnic. People would gather at dusk, enjoy the vendors' offerings and each other, listen to a band concert, and retreat for home about 10:00 P.M.

Saturday's celebration started with a parade at 1:00 P.M. in the afternoon. The parade included decorated floats from local merchants and organizations, visiting bands from Columbia, Valmeyer, Red Bud, and Belleville, and various civic organizations such as the Boy Scouts, Veterans, and PTA, whose marchers carried their banner or message. The auto dealerships would supply the convertibles from which town dignitaries and officials could greet the throng lining the streets. Waterloo's fire engines joined the marchers, with firemen tossing candy to the scrambling children. Farm implement dealerships added their array of tractors to the procession. School aged children would decorate their bicycles with crepe paper and flags, and ride in loose formation in the procession. Many equestrians rode their prized horses, the riders dressed in their finest "western" attire, and the horses outfitted for this occasion with show saddles. The Waterloo Municipal Band was the final feature of the parade, and how grand they were!

Following the parade, all of the band members would gather near the beer stand and receive their well deserved refreshment and get relief from the hot, Illinois, August sunshine.

My grandmother had mixed feelings about Homecoming. Our home became "headquarters" for the out-of-town relatives. But this meant that my grandmother had to put on the "host's dinner," a feast that her sense of protocol demanded. That was hard work, and none of the visiting relatives could help because they were so busy "visiting." But she and my mother prepared a grand dinner that was completed in time for the

Meet My Waterloo *Entertainment*

afternoon parade. And she chose dinner instead of supper for a reason. She was concerned that some of the relatives "stood too close for too long" at the beer stand, and, by late afternoon, they could be quite boisterous and loudly argumentative. Everyone was on his own for supper!

The Capitol Theatre
The ever changing entertainment venue for the town was the Capitol Theatre's movie slate. Each film had approximately a two night run with a 7:00 P.M. and a 9:00 P.M. showing, and a special film directed to children for Sunday matinee.

Saturday and Sunday nights were dedicated to the adults with the more popular Hollywood films and their famous stars being the drawing attraction. The Sunday matinees were tailored to attract the children with double features starring the Three Stooges, Abbot and Costello, the Marx Brothers, Hopalong Cassidy, Roy Rogers, Gene Autry and the like. Action and slapstick! Between features, the theater would present a continuing action serial such as *Captain Midnight* or *Sky King*. Fifteen minutes of intrigue would be presented with the hero always in some precarious situation at the end of that show's segment, inspiring you, of course, to return the next week to see how the escape was accomplished. Occasionally, a short film quiz would be shown providing a timed multiple choice selection race. On other occasions, Movietone News was presented, especially during the war.

"Dish" night was a promotion to encourage regular mid-week movie attendance. The occasion was so named because a set of dishes would be given as a prize to one lucky attendee for that evening. All patrons could register with the theater, and their registration cards were placed in a large cylindrical cage or drum. These cards would stay in the container from week-to-week. After the first show of the evening (between the 7:00 P.M. and 9:00 P.M. "showings"), the cage would be placed on stage in front of the movie screen and some fortunate child was paid a quarter to draw the lucky name. To collect, the winner had to be present at that show. If that person was not present, the prize remained for the drawing the next week.

I remember amazing movies such as the *Wizard of Oz, Bambi,* and *Gone With the Wind.* They were enormously entertaining, shown in color rather than black and white, and not personally threatening. How different it was for movies such as the *Wolf Man, Frankenstein, Dracula, Dr. Jekyll and Mr. Hyde,* the *Picture of Dorian Grey,* or *Phantom of the Opera.* These stories captured your attention through fear. I remember watching the transformation of man to beast in the *Wolf Man,* the transition being so fearsome that I slid down in my seat and watched the awesome event through the crack between the seats, believing I could see the Wolf Man but he couldn't see me! And the end of the picture was no relief. The walk home after dark presented every type of new terror one could imagine. Trees became ogres, shadows hid evil "things," the wind was a breathing monster. I spent as much time looking over my shoulder as looking forward. How wonderful when you scampered into the safe confines of your own home! It was, of course, better to see the scary pictures in summer because neighbors sat in their front yards during the evening, and if they were still there, the "things" certainty were not. In the winter, you were all alone for the long walk home!

Part III
My Education

Chapter 7 Family

Chapter 8 School

Chapter 9 Church

Lloyd and Grandma

Chapter 7   Family

Family, from a child's point of view, just happened to you -- you lived with what you got issued. My most influential family members consisted of my paternal grandmother, my parents, and a favorite uncle. My grandfathers were not a known family presence; my maternal grandfather died six years before I was born, and my paternal grandfather, when I was three. My grandmothers, on the other hand, lived long lives with my maternal grandmother living to one hundred-and-one years old, and my paternal grandmother to eighty-three. Both grandmothers therefore had ample opportunity to have an influence on me, although at different stages of my life.

My mother was a gentle person, and she provided most of the impetus for my religious upbringing and formal education. When my mother returned to work in the early 1940s, I was left during the day under "Grandma's" care and Grandma became a significant influence. My father, being the primary income provider, was away from home much of the time. There was always a "distance" between my father and me, and it was only occasionally that he directly influenced my life. More available to me, Uncle Wilbur was my major male role model and became, by default, my surrogate father, although I do not believe either of us realized it at the time. I had many wonderful aunts, uncles, and cousins, and I enjoyed the kinship they provided, but they were close relatives, not influential "family" as were my mother, Grandma, and Uncle Wilbur.

Grandma
My paternal grandparents, Emma and Arthur Engelbrecht, appeared to have a reasonably comfortable life and loving relationship. My grandmother was small (four feet ten inches), and was always a desired dance partner. She met Arthur at a dance. Their romance flourished, and they were married in 1899. They raised their three sons, Wilbur, Robert, and my father, George, in Waterloo.

A financial setback around 1920 interfered with their plans for the timely completion of their own home, but with the help of their sons, they did finish building the house that I call home, around 1925. Arthur was still working at the mill when he died in 1935, and after that, income for my grandmother ceased. As a result of Arthur's death, and because of the Depression, my parents and I moved in with my grandmother Emma. Grandma Engelbrecht was, from that time on, a personal family member, not a relative. When I said "Grandma," it was she that I addressed; that was her name, not just her position.

One certainly recognized a powerful work ethic in Grandma! No matter how difficult the tasks, she would tackle everything. She could tend the furnace, decapitate a turkey, climb a tall ladder to pick the highest cherries, can bushels of fruit and vegetables, paint the porch, and cultivate the huge vegetable and flower garden. If the job needed doing, she led the way. However, she was also fairly clever at the art of making you "want" to help with the work she undertook. She had no reservations about letting everyone know how hard she worked, and implied that if we really loved her, she would not have to do all the work. In general, she would make anyone within earshot know she felt overworked and under appreciated. Her quest for sympathy made anyone nearby feel like a miserable ingrate, no matter how much of a workload you, also, were carrying. The psychology certainly worked on me, and throughout my youth, I would look for as many jobs around the house as I could handle just to keep her from attempting them and thereby making me feel guilty. Perhaps she did not use the best teaching technique, but I did learn to look for tasks, not wait to be told. I suspect this was the way the work ethic was brought into *her* life and to those of prior generations.

Grandma was a very loving grandmother to her grandson. On a hot summer afternoon, there was always the cold pitcher of Kool-Aid stirred up just for us (just me?). Crackers with sweetened peanut butter, or radish sandwiches were frequent treats. For picnics, there was often a quarter slipped into my pocket as spending money. If I misbehaved, she handled the punishment and did not "snitch" to my parents. I always carried the knowledge that she cared about me and for me.

There were other precious lessons to be learned from her. She had a town-wide reputation for having a beautiful flower garden. And how she enjoyed the garden and that reputation! But she was not the only one who was renowned for flowers. One of her very good friends, Marie Osterhage, also had such a reputation, and the two of them would frequently call on each other, inspect the garden, and have their afternoon visit conducted in Low Deutsche. How frustrated she could be when she discovered that Marie had greater success with a specific flower than she did! Frustrated, yes, angry, no. They remained the best of friends and competitors. One did not get angry or show dismay over having been bettered; you congratulated the victor. Nor did you gloat or strut when you clearly had a greater success than your competitor. Win or lose, each had to walk away with honor and respect. What a tutelage at my early age from this tiny woman! While I have often failed to apply this lesson, even today it can drift into my memory after I find myself regretting my response to some situation.

Mom

My mother was the oldest of six children, and was sent to work in the knitting mills as soon as she graduated from grade school. Her income went directly to help support the large family, especially after her father died in 1925 when she was sixteen years old. Her earnings, along with her mother's income as a seamstress and cleaning lady, fed the family of seven. This difficult beginning left her reticent to discuss her life with anyone, at least while I was young. But I discovered later she was yearning to talk about her life. It was only after I had grown up that I learned that she and my father eloped so she could escape the captivity of her early existence. What joy she had telling me the story of their elopement from Waterloo and Chester, and their train ride to Chicago to be married the next day, only to find out the marriage license bureau was closed because of Columbus Day! She laughed with great delight as she pointed out that they were married "a day later (*not* a day late)!"

Her life for the ten years following my birth was one of submission. Her role as a wife was to serve her husband, and her role as mother was to nurture me. Once settled in her mother-in-law's home, she remained respectfully silent about household management, and deferent to the matriarchal head. How liberated she felt when she returned to work in the 1940s and began to enjoy her identity outside the home! To her credit, she hid her tribulations of family conflict from me until I was old enough to understand.

It was inevitable that a strong Lutheran mother and a cavalier Catholic father would eventually have a confrontation on the subject of my upbringing. Before their marriage, my mother elicited a promise from my father that their children would be raised Lutheran, and he agreed. Little did each of them know that when they moved to Waterloo, the Lutheran minister and the school systems would be thorns in their sides. When it was time for me to enter first grade, the Lutheran school was a one-room schoolhouse with one teacher, who was also the minister. My father had little respect for him, but he kept his promise. When it came time for me to enter the second grade, a new public school opened, with a teacher for each grade. Now my father asserted his will and insisted that I go to the public school. My mother acquiesced this time, with the condition that I return to the Lutheran school for the seventh and eighth grades, to complete my requirement for Confirmation. What an effect these decisions had on me! While the shuffle between the schools was disruptive to my social life, I did receive the opportunity to extract the best from each style of education. And the valuable experience of the one-room school would have been lost, were it not for my mother's strong will.

Uncle Wilbur
Voids seem to get filled. My father, for his own reasons, was relatively unavailable to me during my youth. Uncle Wilbur had not yet married, and he loved children. We more or less adopted each other; he became my surrogate father, and I, his surrogate son. This relationship lasted until his own son, Dale, arrived in the early 1940s.

Uncle Wilbur, a commercial artist, worked and lived in St. Louis. But he loved his home town of Waterloo. Several weekends a month, he would return to enjoy this town, be with his friends, and enjoy fishing. On many of his excursions, I was invited to be his companion. Wilbur was an avid photographer and he and I photographed Fountain Creek, a small stream that meanders through the county. He used every opportunity to help me appreciate the beauty of this natural landscape.

My uncle was an avid fisherman, and he was especially fond of fishing at Beaver Lake, a pond south of Waterloo. The pond was used by a fishing club that had equipped the nearby clubhouse with a coal stove, several cots, card tables and chairs. Angling for catfish (our favorite) began at sunset and continued until the early hours of the morning, or until we caught the limit. Then, the cots provided a place to sleep for

Meet My Waterloo   *Family*

both of us until sunrise, when he would begin fly-fishing for bass while I continued to sleep.

Many a night we sat in the rowboat while fishing, marveling at the wonders of the sky. He was a treasury of information on astronomy, science, and folklore, and the clear country air exposed the heavens in all their splendor for us to explore. How many "what ifs" we evaluated, and how many thought-provoking mysteries we pursued! "What happened before the beginning of time?" "What's on the outside of the outer reaches of space?" And of course, the fun was in the formulation of such profound questions that we knew we could not answer! And all the while we would catch catfish, listen to the frogs croak their mating calls, watch fireflies, see the moon rise, witness the bats and owls conducting their evening hunt, and once in awhile, see a meteor. In this arrangement of companionship and mutual support, my uncle taught me the fun of sports and the marvels of nature.

One of my most memorable lessons from him was delivered in the early 1940s. Wilbur came to Waterloo when he heard that his brother Robert had died. Both he and my father were dutifully present to console my grandmother and comfort her with their strength during her grief. After dark, Wilbur said to me, "Let's go sit in the car," and once we were there, he wept openly. It was then I understood his loss as the oldest brother, and more importantly, that it was okay for a man to cry.

Wilbur married in the early 1940s. His wife Emma accepted my friendship with Wilbur, and occasionally, the three of us went fishing together. Within a few years, they had their son, Dale, and to my surprise, I did not feel jealousy, but rather, the kinship of gaining a surrogate "little brother." How I enjoyed showing him Lloyd's Waterloo as he perched on the handlebars of my bicycle! My family had grown larger!

Washington Hall

Chapter 8   School

Grade school exposed me to two radically different teaching approaches. The public school had a teacher for each grade of approximately thirty children each. Through grade four, one teacher taught all the subjects -- she was your teacher for the year. For grades five through eight, teachers specialized in certain disciplines, one for math, one for history and civics, one for English and grammar, and so forth. The teachers retained their own rooms, and the students moved to the different classrooms to access their full curriculum. Each period of classwork involved only one discipline, and you were not distracted by other classes. How different this experience would be from my first grade introduction to school!

The Lutheran School had only one room in which about thirty students in the eight grades shared the day and the sole teacher. For those in the lower grades, there was a constant exposure to higher grade lessons in every discipline, and I learned far more than expected by the first grade curriculum. Third grade multiplication tables, second grade spelling,

Meet My Waterloo   *School*

seventh grade civics, and fifth grade history were but a few of the "overheard" subjects of my school day. The higher grade students also had advantages (as I learned in seventh and eight grades) in that each class taught at the lower level was a refresher course. Older and more adept students were occasionally assigned to help struggling lower-grade pupils, a rewarding experience for all.

But the one-room school could also be intimidating. Your imperfections at oral reading, arithmetic, and spelling were visible to the whole school, and egregious errors sometimes elicited laughter from the older and wiser students. There was a significant incentive to accomplish your homework in order to minimize the frequency of that problem!

Our school building had an interesting history. Built in the 1800s, "Washington Hall," as it was called, was an inn along the stagecoach route. It was a two-story, sandstone structure with a hallway passing through the middle of the first floor, running front-to-back. On the one side was a large dining room and tavern. Across the hall were several guest rooms for the overnight travelers. The upstairs was a combination dance hall and stage, specifically designed for entertainment. By the 1920s, the inn had outlived its usefulness in that role, and the building was bought by the Lutheran Church for the specific purpose of Christian education. The tavern was converted to a school room and heated with a potbelly stove. The guest rooms across the hall were used for storage of books, desks and tables. The upstairs ballroom was seldom used for school purposes although we were allowed to play our recess games there if it was raining. The ballroom was primarily a meeting room reserved for church social functions such as quilting groups, the Ladies Aid Society, and as the entertainment center for the annual church picnic.

Meet My Waterloo   *School*

The playground for the school consisted of a woods (at least a small park) populated with elm, maple, oak, and hickory trees. It was a difficult place to play baseball or Crack-the-Whip, but ideal for Kick-the-Can, and Hide-and-Seek. Since all grades shared the playground, and there were so few students in each grade, many of the games included participants with widely varying ages. Accommodating a variety of skills associated with the age differences became a playground skill itself. When older children forgot the need for consideration of the younger ones, there was retribution.

One game we played was called the Airplane Ride. An older student would lie down on his back, and raise his legs, knees against his chest. A smaller child would sit on his feet, and then be launched for an airborne trip. On one occasion, I, a skinny little first grader, was the recipient of the ride, but the launcher became too exuberant or miss-judged my weight, and launched me much farther than planned. I crash-landed into the side of a huge maple tree, dropped to the ground, and immediately felt an excruciating pain in my elbow. Wailing in agony, I was taken to the teacher, who determined that the elbow was not broken and the pain would eventually subside.

In the meantime, the whole school assembled in the classroom, and the teacher made an inquiry concerning my misfortune. Three older boys were determined to be "guilty," one because he was the launcher, and the other two because they were co-conspirators. Each was required to bend over the front desk, while a spanking was administered, not because of my injury, but because they did not think about the consequences! Then the minister looked at me, and announced that I would not be spanked because I was already punished

Meet My Waterloo   *School*

enough for being so foolish! Bad day! And my elbow still hurt! And the day wasn't over yet....

I arrived home late in the afternoon, unable to move my arm, my elbow swollen far beyond its normal size. When my father came home and saw the injury, he immediately called the doctor. We were promptly summoned to his office, where the doctor realized that an X-ray was necessary before planning any corrective action. Waterloo doctors did not have a diagnostic X-ray machine, but the dentist did. We were sent to the dentist's office where he devised a makeshift lab. I sat on a three-legged stool, put my arm on the equipment tray between the film plate under my arm and the X-ray head poised just above my elbow. Several exposures were made, and the dentist disappeared to develop the film. While we were waiting, the three legged chair on which I was sitting collapsed, slinging my injured arm over my head. I screamed and cursed the dentist. That was the first time a parent had heard me swear and I fully expected punishment for that "slip," but my father understood. The poor dentist bounced around his office trying to hurry the process so I could return to the doctor. My dislocated elbow was "popped back in," and my arm was placed in a sling. I wallowed in a lot of attention at school the next day, but that was the end of the affair. I reflect now from time to time on the game, the punishment, and the treatment, and smile with amusement at how those events might be handled today.

During the time I was in first grade, the new public school was being built as part of the WPA program, and I was subsequently enrolled there. Now my classmates were all my own age, and for the first time, friendship and bonding started in earnest. Many of these children remained classmates through high school, and are revered friends to this day.

Meet My Waterloo *School*

But the classes were now highly regimented, with only one subject at a time. There was no competing or enlightening curriculum from different levels, and individual attention was greatly reduced. While I did very well in this environment, I mostly remember my friends and teachers, not the curriculum.

As required, I returned to the Lutheran School and Washington Hall for seventh grade. It was expected that children planning to be confirmed in the church attend seventh and eighth grades at the school in order to receive the proper religious training. The school had changed very little, but it did have a furnace now. The teacher was still the minister, but he had mellowed a little -- or at least I perceived that because I now knew him better as my friend Roland's father.

Since the minister's residence and the school were adjacent to each other, Roland, around noon, would be sent to the mailbox across the street to retrieve the mail. One day he rushed back in and yelled "Fire!" Seeing the panic in our eyes, the teacher ordered us to sit still while he investigated. Within seconds, he returned, and calmly instructed us to leave and assemble across the street. The desks we used were the side arm type with a storage area under the seat, and writing space along the right side arm. You stored all your possessions such as caps, coat, books, tablets, baseball gloves, or anything else that was yours in that storage space. How everyone gasped when I emerged from the room dragging and shoving my desk down the steps and across the street! No fire was going to get my possessions!

Once across the street, my heart sank as I looked back at the school. Flames had already consumed a section of the wooden shake roof, and could be seen eating their way through the ballroom ceiling. The fire siren screamed its message: "Ward

Meet My Waterloo   *School*

Four," and soon, the wail of the fire engine could be heard. We were hustled away to make room for the firemen who fought the difficult blaze, and, surprisingly, contained the fire to the upper floor. But the entire school building was ruined by water; the basement was half-full of water with the acrid odor of burnt wood, the schoolroom's floorboards were buckled and warped, and the ceiling was devoid of large chunks of soggy plaster much of which had fallen on the desks. The end of Washington Hall!

After the fire, the minister and his family moved to a nearby rental house, and a temporary school was devised using the minister's vacant residence. A foundation was quickly poured on nearby church property, and the minister's house moved to that location. We students crowded into the makeshift schoolroom, completing our education there under the new circumstances.

In the meantime, the minister bought the damaged property and its land from the church, razed the remains of Washington Hall, and used the recovered sandstone to face his new home. The demolished structure also had a large amount of brick that could be used in the new home, so he employed us students (if we desired to work) to clean old mortar from the bricks at a penny a brick. Where else could you go to school, get an education, work at recess, and get paid by the teacher?

Immanuel Lutheran Church

Chapter 9   Church

During the early 1900s, services at Immanuel Lutheran Church were conducted in German. Later, one English service per month was initiated. Now, in the 1930s, there was one German service per month, and there were two services in English every Sunday, with Sunday School taught between the services. The solitary German service was attended by an older generation of townspeople, mostly women, who were frail, stooped, and adorned in widows' black shawls. The old-world traditions of the emigrants from Germany were fading.

Meet My Waterloo *Church*

The church itself was a tiny building, with a small entry way that served as the belfry supporting the modest church steeple. A solitary bell occupied the belfry, and it was rung using a rope dangling through the ceiling. The main part of the structure held two rows of pews, about seven on a side. A potbelly stove was located on the one side of the aisle separating the rows, and the pew next to the stove was, of necessity, a short one. The stove was the only source of heat in the winter, and because of the high ceiling, parishioners had two choices of warmth, shiver or burn! Sitting next to the stove exposed you to the unbearable radiant heat, but if you sat some distance away, the stove did little good because its heat was convected to the ceiling. The stove had to be tended during service, so the caretaker would "fire it up" while the hymns were being sung, but never during the liturgy, and especially never during the sermon!

Your eye, if not captured by the potbelly stove, was certainly attracted to the organ located on the right side of the altar. The organ was there from my earliest memory and I have no knowledge of its origin, but it must have been installed before electrical energy was prevalent. Beside the organ, behind a closed curtain, there was a hand pump that could be employed to pressurize the tank used as the air source for the organ pipes. An electric motor had been installed to provide the air pressure, but if there was a power failure, the hand pump became activated. Unfortunately, insufficient training in its use by the drafted pumpers resulted in limited success. The pump needed to be exercised for some period of time before a sufficient reserve of air was stored to smoothly operate the organ. Because the hand pump made so much noise, it was not allowed to compete with the minister's liturgy, and because one could hear the poor parishioner solicited as the pumper gasping in exhaustion, the pump was operated only while music was playing. Without an adequate reserve of air pressure, each stroke of the handpump modulated the music -- loud on the downstroke, weak on the upstroke. I still remember Martin Luther's hymn:

> "A **mighty fortress** is **our God**,
> A trusty **shield** and weapon,"

the organ would warble as the organist tried her utmost to counter the sound surges with her foot-operated volume control. Martin never heard it like that!

The choir sat in the first two rows facing the organ. The choir was staffed by draftees and volunteers, and singing quality was not among the criteria for selection. I was drafted, and hated it! I knew I did not qualify, therefore I sang as softly as I could. Furthermore, you had to *really* behave, being up in front of the congregation, and near the minister. Because of our variable degrees of skill, and the frequent disasters when someone sang both loudly and off key, the choir became timid, and could hardly be heard. To make matters worse, no time could be agreed on (and complied with) for practice, so rehearsal was limited to a few minutes before the parishioners were let in for the church service. The *Introit* and *Gradual* were always surprises to us. Out of mercy, the organist played loudly to drown out our mistakes. But my mother was happy. Her son was in the choir!

There were two special services that I remember vividly, one was held annually on Christmas Eve, and the other, once in your lifetime -- your Confirmation. On Christmas Eve, all of the school-aged children were required to perform in the service. The children were seated in the front pews and arranged, to the extent possible, to permit their orderly participation in the program. The lights would be dimmed to emphasize the Christmas tree, and, group-by-group, and age-by-age, the children would step upon the altar platform, face the congregation, and, child-by-child, recite his or her "piece" of some well known Christmas passage from the Bible. Learning your "piece" was vital since you recited that alone. You trudged up to, and raced down from, the platform. In between speaking parts, you had some relief because hymns were sung, some with the congregation, some by the children's choirs. During the service, the minister would deliver a very short sermon directed to the children. Each and every step of the program emphasized the Christian reason for the Christmas celebration, and we understood. The service ended with "Silent Night," of course, and as we filed out of the church, each child received a paper bag of hard candy.

Sunday school was also directed at the education of children, and was tailored for some of the curriculum needed for Confirmation. Each Sunday, between the two services, the "teaching" corps would take their charges and work with them in separate groups. The corps was made up of volunteers, many of whom had children in the classes. The Sunday School teachers were briefed weekly by the minister for their hour long sessions with the students. As seventh and eighth graders being groomed for Confirmation, we were given special instruction by the minister. These classes could actually be enjoyable because they fostered discussion, with the minister posing questions, and we the students being encouraged to speculate on answers or solutions. One such lesson that I remember considered the idea of committing what *you* believed to be a sin, but, in the eyes of the church, the act was not sinful (the example was adult smoking). The question was, "If you engage in the act, are you committing a sin?" My answer: "Yes, because you intended to sin." Even I was surprised by this intellectual enlightenment of being able to separate the intent from the act. But I topped that! The question was asked if people knew when they were committing a sin. All agreed, "Yes." "Then why do it?" he asked. "Because sinning is fun," I blurted out. My peers gasped that I would make such a "confession," but the minister nearly choked with laughter while beaming with pride. Now he had evidence he had gotten through to at least one of his "kids."

Confirmation is a ritual inflicted on the innocent to make them grateful they will never have to go through the process again. For two years, doctrine is drilled into your conscious and subconscious minds until you know the right answer to everything. Then you have to prove it! One Sunday morning, nine of you are lined up in front of the congregation, and grilled. There was no set order to the person selected to respond to each inquiry, therefore you had to know it all. "Please, God, no mental lapses now!" Elation when you answered correctly, apprehension waiting for your next turn. Then, as if you had not been subjected to enough torture, your class had to sing "their class hymn" selected by the minister. Lutherans do not believe in Purgatory, but they have Confirmation to take its place, and it happens to you while you are alive!

Part IV
Home

Chapter 10   The Kitchen

Chapter 11   The Attic

Chapter 12   The Cherry Tree

Chapter 13   My Shed

Chapter 14   The Basement

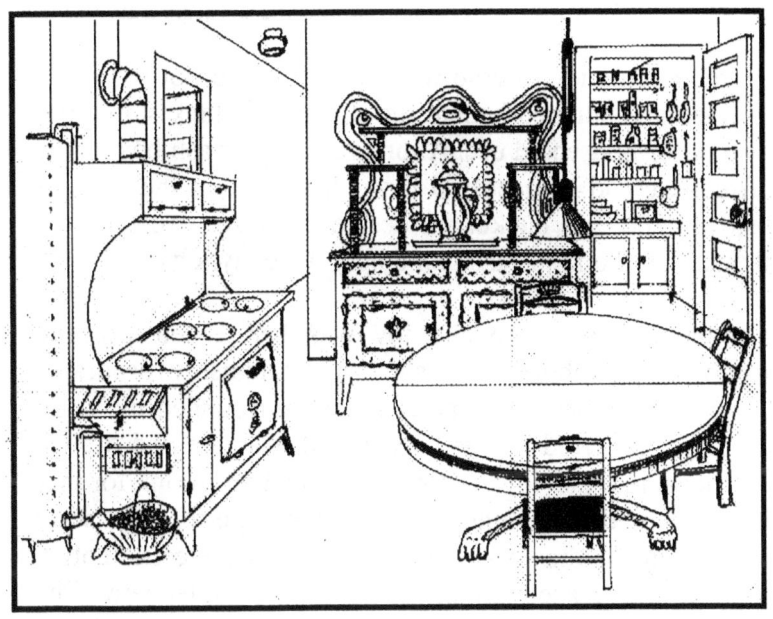

The Kitchen

Chapter 10   The Kitchen

Home life centered around the kitchen. In winter, it was the warmest and most comfortable room in the house. Cooking, eating, homework, hobbies, knitting, and socializing all took place here. The most important fixture in the room was the coal fired stove that was used for cooking year round, and was the mainstay for heat in the winter. Its oven door and face plates were sky blue enamel, its top, black, and the trim was chromium steel. The fire was kindled in the early morning, and continued until bedtime. Round stove lids were removable to allow cleaning soot from the stove's interior. Grates on the side of the firebox permitted air regulation to the glowing embers. Warming chambers were located above the stove's cooking surface and used to maintain the warmth of prepared food until it was served. A water jacket lined the firebox to allow the circulation of cold water in from, and hot water out to, a steel tank situated behind the stove. This tank stored our hot water for household use. A long rectangular ash box below the firebox could be accessed through a door on the front of the stove. The coal bucket sat beside the stove. Keeping the coal bucket full and the ash box empty were my jobs.

My grandmother's pride and joy was her "sideboard," an ornate wooden cabinet with shelves outlandishly decorated with wooden embellishments. A mirror surrounded by wood filigree was centered on the back board. Cabinet and drawer space occupied the lower portion, providing room for her dishware behind the cabinet doors, and storage for silverware and linens in the drawers. Her treasured silver electric coffee percolator was placed on the center of the sideboard. The sideboard was painted sky blue to match the dominant color of the stove. This monstrosity was silently disliked by the other adults, having bruised many a hip on its protruding corners. It was liked even less when my grandmother decided to refinish it with grass green colored paint. I did not have an opinion; it was just one of those artifacts present since the day you arrived -- part of the house.

A round "clawfoot" table occupied the center of the room. It was large enough to seat four adults and me, and we ate every meal at this table unless we had company. Four "tea-rose" chairs surrounded the table at mealtime. Chappie occupied the position opposite the sideboard; my father was on his right; my mother sat next to the sideboard, and my grandmother was seated next to the stove. I sat between my mother and grandmother, first on a high step stool, and later, on a regular chair. The position was selected when I was a youngster needing help to cut my food, and the position stuck throughout

Meet My Waterloo   *The Kitchen*

childhood. It became my personal territory -- I even worked on my homework there.

The pantry was located next to the sideboard. It was the room with good smells! All foodstuffs for imminent use were stored in the pantry, and with the mixture of spices, cookies and cakes, one could work up a hunger quickly. Flour, sugar, baking powder, and salt were stored in metal tins. Bread had its place in a bread box, a semi-airtight container used to lengthen bakery products' freshness. Hooks and nails were pounded into every convenient location to hang cooking pots, frying pans, roasting pans, spatulas, meat forks, measuring spoons, and racks. Cooking equipment such as the "regular" coffee pot, toaster, and Mixmaster were allocated shelf space. The pantry was originally built to operate as a cooler, with the top of the cupboard designed as a sink with a soldered lining to make it watertight. The intent was to be able to circulate cool water through the sink, keeping foods requiring only modest refrigeration safe to eat.

In the summer, the icebox was placed near the rear wall of the kitchen facing the side of the stove. In the winter, it was moved outside to the enclosed back porch to permit the cold outside air to furnish much of the refrigeration.

The sink was located in the corner of the kitchen, near Chappie's position. This porcelain fixture was open on all sides, the exposed plumbing covered with a small curtain.

Only one light served the entire kitchen. It hung from the approximate center of the room and resembled the kind of illumination you would see over a pool table. The green conical shade covered a light bulb, and the fixture could be raised or lowered on a counter-weighted pulley system.

During meals, when a wide area of light was needed, the light was raised. When I worked on homework, it was lowered to provide sufficient light for my reading and writing. Anyone else wanting to read or write without eyestrain, had to sit close to me.

In the winter, the family would gather in the kitchen after supper. I would work on my homework, my grandmother would knit, and my mother would sew or write letters. Occasionally she would join my father, reading the newspaper. Some nights, I was required to have my homework done early, since a family favorite radio program would be turned on, but only if my homework was completed. I much preferred listening to the *Lux Radio Theater* and *Major Bowes' Amateur Hour* to doing homework, so by (my) definition, it was done when these programs came on.

As bedtime approached, my grandmother would tend her flowers. Each window sill was lined with potted plants which thrived on their dose of afternoon sunshine. The windows, however, provided only minimal protection from the cold winter nights, with "hoarfrost" decorating the inside of the windowpanes regularly, so Grandma would place a barrier between the window and plants using pieces of cardboard as insulators. Then towels, used as blankets, would be placed over the plants. Finally, she would "bank the fire," an expression used to describe the process of covering a fire with ashes so that glowing embers would last through the night and could be used to help rekindle the fire in the morning. Her grandson would then get his nightly hug, and be off to bed.

The kitchen is the place I fondly remember where we had joyful family time that included my parents, Grandma, and me. It was the daily family gathering place for supper, the

Meet My Waterloo   The Kitchen

family room for nightly projects, and the assembly room for radio listening. It was the place of good smells that began with meal preparation, and lingered long after the dishes were done. In winter, it was the cozy, warm room that drew everyone near the stove. When I wanted companionship, the kitchen was the place to be.

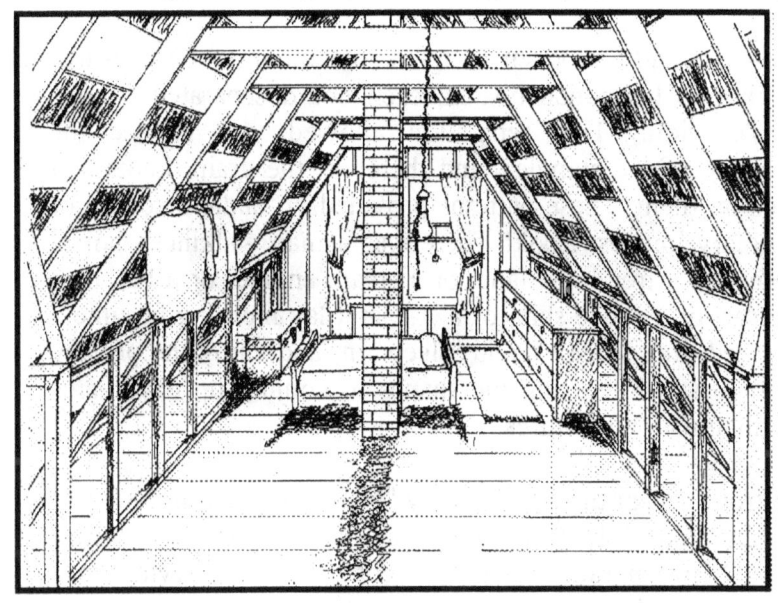

The Attic

Chapter 11   The Attic

The kitchen was a "public" place. The attic, however, could be my private and fantasy domain, especially on Saturday mornings. Due to financial constraints, my grandparents could not finish the upstairs level of the home. As a result, the upstairs, or attic as I called it, consisted of one large, naked room. The rafters and underside of the roof were exposed and had no insulation or plaster. Chimneys were located near the front and back of the attic, the front serving the furnace, the back venting the kitchen and basement laundry stoves. Dormers on either side of the gabled roof provided additional floor space and head room.

The house had a wooden shingled roof mounted on one-inch by six-inch horizontal boards, each board separated by one board's width. This separation allowed you to see the underside of the shingles, and therefore the grain, knots and stains on them. These patterns provided an endless source of imaginary images. Look! There was a man walking a horse. There was a tree-lined lane, or a steam engine, or a bat, or a race car, or a space ship, or a .... Saturday morning became a treasured time since I could "sleep" in, and enjoy the privacy of my attic while using the shapes to conjure up daydreams and imaginary adventures.

The front part of the attic was my "bedroom." It was equipped with an antique chest of drawers, an old steamer trunk, a wire strung between rafters that held coat hangers (serving as a closet), and, of course, my bed. Over time, I had several beds. My first was an old army cot padded with a "corn shuck" mattress. Although the mattress rustled as you moved in the bed, it was comfortable. The two-foot thick bag of corn stalk leaves compressed to just a few inches under your body, but a protective "wall" remained around the sides. This was a distinct advantage in the winter. This arrangement had only one drawback, and that was the sagging of the cot. It was closer to sleeping in a hammock than a bed. The cot was later replaced by a bed with a more supportive understructure, but the corn shuck mattress remained. The bed was placed next to the chimney since its bricks gave off some warmth in the winter.

The attic was a great place to sleep in the summer. Although it became extremely hot in the afternoon, it would cool to a comfortable temperature in the evening. You could lie next to the open windows and feel the cooling night breeze, listen to the nighttime sounds of crickets and frogs, hear the singing of tires as trucks sped into town on Route 3, and best of all, hear the trains.

You had to be persistent to gain an advantage from the prevailing breeze. When the breeze came from the west (the usual case), my "bedroom" at the front of the attic was the place to be. In addition to permitting the cooling draft of air, the window allowed the streetlight to play shadow games through the sycamore trees that lined Main Street, and project dancing forms on the ceiling. Also, the singing of truck tires was delightfully prominent. However, when the air movement was from the north or south, it was far better to sleep in a dormer. I would drag my cot to the south dormer, where I could capture the benefit of this reoriented breeze. This location made it far easier to hear the trains. One could also see the flash of light on the attic wall from the aircraft beacon located north of town -- a burst of white as the thin beam swung around, and, seconds later (if you watched carefully), the blink of green. On many nights, that beacon triggered a "daydream" of flying an airplane, only to have the adventure drift into sleep.

For a long time, I had no preference for the location of my bed. Each position had its benefits. That changed! One year, a local contractor was building several houses, one at the south end of town, another on the vacant lot directly next door (and adjacent to the south dormer). Supposedly, he was having labor difficulties, and there was a subsequent suspicious explosion at the distant construction site. Fearing a replication of that event at the job site next door, I, as a youth, never slept in the south dormer again.

It was pleasant to go to bed in the summer. But the winter was another story. The attic was not insulated and there was also no provision to supply it with heat. If it was bitter cold outside, it was bitter cold upstairs. No longer could you have the windows open to hear the night sounds, lest the cold wind further aggravate your problem of warmth. Going to bed meant donning warm pajamas, dashing across the cold floor, springing into bed as you covered your entire body with the layers of blankets, and gently wiggling your body against the bed sheets to donate all the body heat you could to warm the bed. On nights of extreme cold, a brick, warmed in the kitchen stove oven and wrapped in a towel, accompanied you to bed to keep your feet warm. Before long, you could become quite comfortable, and you could dare to expose your nose to the crisp air. Once you were warmly buried in the mound of blankets, sleep would come quickly. But then, you faced a new problem in the morning!

The church bells that announced morning mass served as the alarm clock that ordered me to get up. Now the temperature was even lower than when you went to bed, and how awful the prospect of leaving that warm comfortable bed for the cold dash to downstairs' warmth. On several occasions, snow dusted my bed, having slipped into the attic through a crack between the roofline and the chimney next to my bed. On these mornings, the prospects were even more foreboding. It took fortitude, and occasionally, some parental coaxing, to make that daring sprint.

The Back Yard

Chapter 12   The Cherry Tree

"...Climb up my ~~apple~~ cherry tree..." There was a wonderful cherry tree located in my back yard. Its lower branches were fortuitously placed at a height that permitted me to climb the tree, even when I was very young. Its upper branches had sufficient foliage that I could be hidden from view while exploring. Branches were plentiful and well placed so that I had ladder-like access to the whole tree. Various forks in the trunk provided space for seats, a make-believe dash board, and control sticks for airplanes, rocket ships, and race cars. Since one was high above the ground, it was truly like being airborne -- one could see over the lilac bushes and grape arbor, which became pretend mountains or forest.

When friends were not available for play, I would escape to the cherry tree. Climbing to the higher branches shielded me from view from the house, and permitted me to believe the house was not near. Little did I know that I was totally exposed because each fantasy was accompanied by my oral sound effects -- **"vaarrrrrooom"** for airplanes, **"ssswwhooshhhh"** for rocket ships, **"ack-ack-ack-ack-ack"** for machine guns, and the prize winning **"sssccccrrrreeeeechhh"** for squealing tires. This fantasy action was, of course, accompanied by body contortions commensurate with the terrible G-forces experienced on those missions, but only once did I fall. I slid part way down a high limb, dropped onto branch after branch, and finally thudded to the ground, dazed. My arms, chest, back and legs were scratched and I had a lump on my forehead. But no one had seen me fall, therefore I did not have to be embarrassed. Gingerly, I crawled back into the airplane to nurse my wounds before taking off on another mission. The misguided fantasy lasted until I was called in for supper, and did I "catch it" for not reporting into sick bay!

During the late summer, you could always land your aircraft, taxi up to the grape arbor, and feast on Concord grapes. Planted by my grandparents for wine and jelly production, these grape vines were intertwined throughout the arbor, dangling the purple fruit at tempting heights. Since my grandfather was no longer alive to make wine, we had more grapes than my grandmother could convert to grape jelly, and therefore, grapes were always available as a snack. How delicious they were! One would just tug on a cluster, rinse it at the cistern pump, and eat. Your path was clearly visible from the trail of grape skins left behind. Then, back to the ~~cherry tree~~ airdrome.

Meet My Waterloo   *The Cherry Tree*

The cistern was a vital part of my adventures. Almost every house in the community had a way of collecting water without depending on the Waterloo Water Company. Each home had either a cistern or a well. Wells were shafts that were dug sufficiently deep to intercept underground springs. As the urban population grew, the limited water supply of the wells was inadequate for the town, and therefore wells were principally used by the farmers. Cisterns were large underground storage tanks, made of concrete or stone, and used to store rainwater. The roofline of our house had rain-gutters that led to downspouts. These downspouts drained either into the cistern or a drainage ditch. The first few rains of the spring were always "wasted" into the ditch to permit the rainwater to rinse the roof and clear away the winter's dirt and soot. But later, the water was directed into the cistern for storage. This water, being mineral free, was called "soft" water. In addition to being used for drinking, it was used for the laundry (it "soaped up" well), and used by women to wash their hair. (Women loved the soft feeling the water imparted to their hair, but for men, it left the hair "wild" and you had to use that "sticky stuff" to regain control.) Since the water was stored underground, the water remained somewhat cool, and was delicious to drink on a hot summer's day.

The cistern pump consisted of a long loop of chain draped over a ratchet wheel driven by the hand crank. The chain had rubber washers on it spaced about three feet apart. The chain was looped through a pipe that extended to the bottom of the cistern. The bottom end was therefore continuously in water. As the chain entered the pipe on its way up, it would trap all the water ahead of the washer which could then be brought up to a small holding tank. The tank was, in turn, emptied by the spigot. A cup hung on a wire hook beside the pump, and everybody drank using that cup. The cranking action created a loud racket, much to the delight of visiting children. They would crank fast and long to make noise and splash water, but fortunately, I could usually stop them before Grandma would storm out of the house. The cistern was no toy!

The cistern was, of course, my imaginary "gas/fuel" station for my adventures. My spacecraft made many a landing to refuel. But the real reason for the stop was to partake of that nourishing water, especially since your throat could get so dry making all those sounds!

The Shed

Chapter 13   My Shed

Well, not really mine, but I was given free use of "the shed," so mentally it became mine. Furthermore, I was left to my own devices there, so I was totally in control -- that too makes it mine. My uncle Robert was an architect in the Engineering Corps during World War I, and upon resuming civilian life, he acquired surplus barracks material to build a small studio for his architectural business in Waterloo. The studio was located behind the garage and in front of the "outhouse,"[5] and was equipped with electricity, but not heat or water.

Robert left Waterloo and the studio became a storage shed. Years later, it was cleared out so that I could use it as a place to play, but it soon took on greater significance. While the attic was my dream space and the cherry tree my fantasy land, the shed became my center for real and stimulating experiments, and projects of many kinds. Here, I dealt with reality.

The shed was about the size of a household room, had windows on two sides, large double doors in front, and a small storage closet on the inside. The original work surface and draftsman's storage drawers had been moved to the house basement for tool storage and workbench space. I therefore built work benches around the inside, the quality of which reflected the abilities associated with my age at the time. Many times I removed old benches to replace them with more sophisticated versions indicative of my advanced age and improved skill.

Initially, the shed was used by me strictly for play on rainy days. Playing outdoors was much more fun, so only inclement weather "drove" us to the shed. Later, however, it became a place to learn and try new concepts. The field of radio seemed interesting, so after reading some literature about the subject, I collected old, broken radios from neighborhood attics, and rebuilt them into (sometimes) working models. Antennae of various configurations sprung up around the yard, stretched from birdhouse to garage to grape arbor to shed, all without a lightning arrester. Crystal radios gave way to tube sets, earphones surrendered to speakers. Conventional domestic broadcast stimulated expansion to world-wide short wave radio. And so my experiments grew as I grew.

Later, I took an interest in chemistry. This was prompted by my receiving a chemistry set from my uncle Wilbur, and I performed every experiment described in the accompanying manual. Now my interest was really piqued! Reading about chemistry led to acquiring chemistry equipment from Hamacher's Pharmacy. Used beakers, flasks, test tubes, glass tubing, corks, and best of all, outdated chemicals became mine, free. Now I began this chemistry business in earnest. Experiment after experiment was conducted, some successful, some not, but I learned from each one. Friends would come to participate (when you conduct experiments, it is no longer "play," it is "participation") in the adventure. One day we attempted to make nitroglycerin. Whether we succeeded or not is not clear. All I can remember is that the experiment "ran away," that is, began boiling more vigorously even after the heat source was removed. Fearing an explosion, we grabbed the double boiler flask setup with a sack, ran to the next door neighbor's yard and dumped the angry liquid. To try to hide the evidence, we lit the mixture, and it burned with an eerie blue flame. No more of that!

Other interests came and went. Wood burning sets delighted the artist in me. A wood-turning lathe was fun for a while, but you could only create cylindrical things and that became boring. However, as my companions and I grew older, new kinds of interests arose. One consisted of making a "Turkish" bath in which one could "cleanse" tobacco pipe smoke in water. (We felt this would keep us from getting discovered because of smoker's breath.) Another interest was our secreted copies of the *Police Gazette*. Each time I see a certain movie actress, I remember her pose in the *Gazette* in a bikini. Pretty risqué for those times! These magazines and the tobacco products were safeguarded in a secret place, the shed's attic, accessed only through an overhead sliding trap door.

The shed was a wonderful stimulus for interesting experimentation, and some of my friends got into trouble because of our level of concentration. On a few occasions, using electric lighting and having an interesting project in progress, we lost track of time. My family, of course, knew where I was, but my friends' parents did not always know of their sons' activities. While parents were often angry over the fact that we appeared inconsiderate, there was still much relief that we were safe at my home and engaged in wholesome (usually) activity. They had feared much worse.

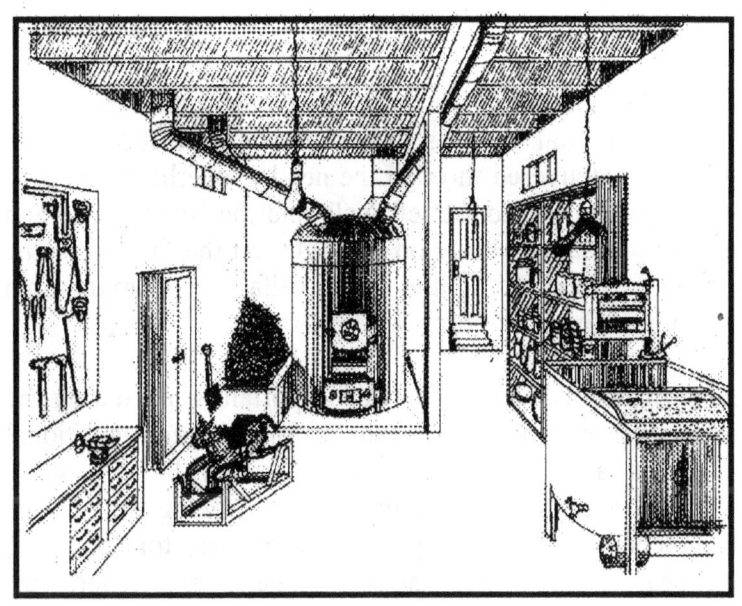

The Basement

Chapter 14   The Basement

The basement served as overflow work space for the family. It was the dedicated place for laundry and household repairs. But it had other roles depending on the time or circumstances. It was used as the winter drying room for laundry and as the furnace room. In summer, it provided ample room for canning and was always a place of cool refuge from the oppressive afternoon heat. In autumn, it became the winery (when my grandfather was alive). For me, my rocking horse was stabled there, and my few toys waited patiently for me on a set of shelves.

The basement was made of poured concrete set into the ground, with sufficient height above ground to permit four narrow windows to let in the outside light. In the center of the basement stood the "Monster," a coal fired furnace that would

Meet My Waterloo *The Basement*

rumble when the wind produced a strong draft through its chimney. The coal bin was located next to the furnace, and this fuel was delivered through the nearby, overhead window. A workbench occupied the left wall, and the laundry area and canned goods storage were on the right. At the far end of the basement, a door led to the "fruit cellar," a storage room located under the front porch.

Canning fruits and vegetables was important work during the summer. It provided us the means of financial and nutritional survival on a Depression budget. A small laundry stove located on a near wall served as the cooking source for canning cherries, apricots, peaches, tomatoes, tomato juice, beets, peas, beans, corn, carrots, cabbage, and sauerkraut. Grape jelly was made in great quantities and used as barter among friends for other delicacies. Tomatoes grow profusely during the Illinois summer, and they were used stewed, sliced, as juice, and in relishes. But tomato juice is tricky. One had to be very thorough in the preparation process or fermentation would take place after bottling. Contents of many exploded tomato juice containers decorated the shelving from time-to-time!

Some fruits and vegetables were not canned, but simply stored in the fruit cellar. Long boards were placed horizontally over the earthen floor, and potatoes, apples, pears, yams, onions, squash, corn, and pumpkins were placed in a single layer on these makeshift shelves. Bruised produce tended to rot, therefore no piece of produce was allowed to touch any other, to prevent cross contamination. Baskets of nuts were also stored here, for use in holiday baking.

Most of the fruit and vegetables were either grown in your own garden or purchased at "bushel" prices from the farmers.

Meet My Waterloo   *The Basement*

As a result, during the summer, fresh produce was always available, with a portion of the produce going directly to the table; the remainder was canned. Basement shelves were used to store these canned goods, thus becoming our local "store." Grocery stores were used for products you could not easily produce for yourselves or buy from the farmers; coffee, sugar, spices, flour, bananas, pineapple, and oranges were in that category. The grocery stores were also used for perishables, such as lettuce and meat, that would not tolerate canning or storage.

For me, the basement was a substitute for my other adventure places during inclement weather. My earliest memory of playing in the basement involves one of the few recollections I have of my grandfather Engelbrecht ("Pom Pom," to me). He had somehow acquired a hobby horse that swung back-and-forth much like the action of "glider swings" familiar to our back yards and porches. He would enjoy pushing the horse for me to ride, and in the process, he would also control the wildness of the horse. Then he would take me to his "crock" to show me the wine he was making. He let me pull the handle of his bottle capper to show me how he stored the wine. "Someday, I'll let you have a sip of hooch," he said. Sadly, we never had that sip together.

The basement was my alternate "shed" in the wintertime, but it had numerous drawbacks. First of all, you had to clean up promptly after (and sometimes, during) a project because the basement was used extensively for laundry and ironing. Additionally, overly "adventurous" projects had to be avoided because of the frequent adult presence. You did not have the same degrees of freedom "down here" that you had "out there," but working in the basement was better than waiting for spring. At least this was one place in the house where you could make a mess!

Part V
Ritual

Chapter 15   Weekly Ritual

Chapter 16   Radio

Chapter 17   Tradition

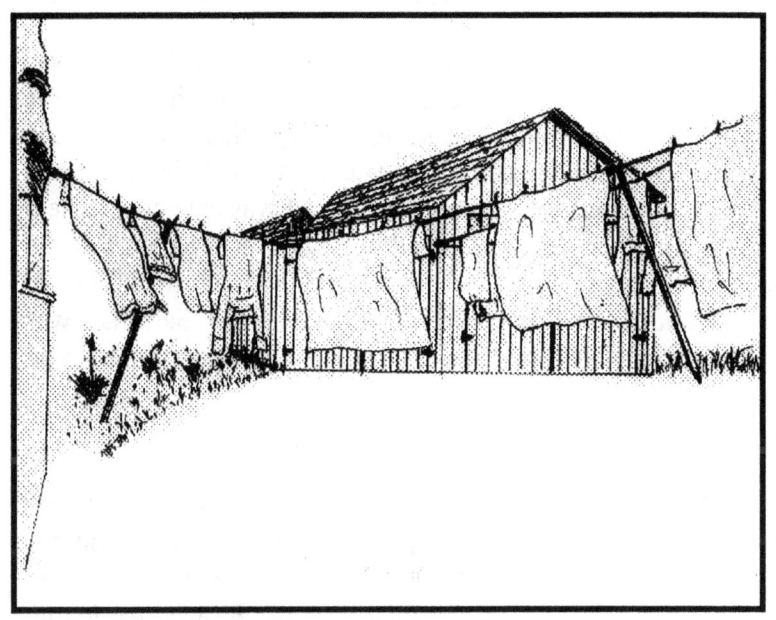

Drying the Laundry

Chapter 15   Weekly Ritual

There was a regularity to each day. Church bells awoke you. The siren beckoned you to dinner at noon and supper at 6:00 P.M. You could hear the passenger train at 7:00 P.M., curfew at 9:00 P.M. In summer, you sat in chairs on the front lawn and conversed with passers-by during the evening hours. In winter, you were trapped indoors, and the evening radio substituted for the lawn chairs.

But it was the weekly agenda that made each day different, with its own theme. For our home, the agenda was primarily set by my grandmother, and her ritual was synchronized with that of others of her generation. Monday was wash day; Tuesday, the ironing was done; Wednesday and Thursday saw gardening and canning; Friday was spent shopping and

Meet My Waterloo   *Weekly Ritual*

baking; Saturday was house cleaning day, and Sunday was reserved for church and company. For me, each day of the school week was much the same as any other, but Saturday was my "chores day," and on Sunday I attended church. When school was closed for summer vacation, I was expected to help my grandmother with her scheduled tasks every day. For the stores and shops, the daily routine of 8:00 A.M. to 6:00 P.M. was extended on Friday until 9:00 P.M., and Saturday was delivery day. Sunday, businesses were closed. Unless you were a tavern!

Monday: Wash Day
There were only a few women of the older generation (by definition, my grandmother's age) that had a reputation for beautiful flowers and garden. But for everyone else, there was no stigma for having an "ordinary" yard. Flower gardening was not considered a "duty." Not so when it came to laundry. If your wash was not absolutely clean, your linens and shirts brilliantly white, and each piece without a wrinkle, you were talked about! "Oh, that poor thing..." the conversation would start, and it made the gossip rounds. My grandmother made sure she never got on that list!

Clothes were first sorted by color, then function, to determine the order of processing. My father's white shirts were always first, white linens, bedsheets and pillow cases next, and so forth through the whites. Then came colored dresses, aprons, towels, and so on until one ended with work pants and play clothes.

The processing ritual was equally rigid. All laundry was boiled "to soften the dirt." Next, the load was hand scrubbed with Fels Naptha bar soap on a wash board and then rinsed in soft water from the cistern, and hand wrung.

The load was now ready for the washing machine! This motorized contraption had a porous cylinder in which the laundry was captured. The drum was immersed in soapy water, and the cylinder spun for a prescribed amount of time. Upon completion of that cycle, the mechanical wringer assembly was swung next to the drum, and the soapy water squeezed from the clothes back into the washing machine, while the load of clothes went into a wash tub. The laundry was thoroughly rinsed by hand until the soap was no longer evident. The wringer assembly was then swung over this rinse tub, and the compression process was repeated as the clothes went into their final processing. This bath contained the "bluing," a chemical ingredient that induced the white clothes to become brilliant white. The wringer was moved to its third position, and the final wringing took place, depositing the clothes into a laundry basket which was used to transport the clothes to the drying area.

This elaborate process was, of course, slow. With one person, only one load could be processed at a time (although another load could be boiling). With two people, the processing time could be significantly reduced. Therefore, my grandmother hired a friend, Barbara Mickenhiemer, to help her. Barbara was a tall, thin, elderly widow. She worked as laundry and house cleaning help wherever she could find work to eke out an existence for herself and her ailing sister. On Mondays and Tuesdays, she worked for my grandmother and joined our family for meals, taking the leftovers home for her sister. My grandmother paid her for her help, but I know the sum was not great. Barbara, however, was so grateful, and enjoyed the time with my grandmother as they spoke in Low Deutsche.

Meet My Waterloo   *Weekly Ritual*

Before my mother started work at the garment factory, she was the third worker, and a regular production line existed. Later, when she worked at the factory, I took that place, at least during summer vacations.

Hanging the clothes to dry was also highly ritualized. Hanging laundry outside was important because it was your means of advertising how competent you were -- the yard was your "show off" place. First the wash line had to be strung in the only open area, which was directly in front of the garage. The line was anchored to the porch, then to the hook on the corner of the garage, back to the corner of the house, then to the middle of the garage, to the flag pole, and finally to the far end of the garage. The line was then wiped clean with a wet towel. Each segment of line had a designated kind of wash it displayed, shirts on the first segment, bed sheets on the second, and so on. Lines that sagged were reinforced with "wash props." These were "one-by-twos," with a notch for the line at the top, and a point to dig into the ground at the other. My grandmother was short, and needed a step ladder to hang the wash. Barbara, being quite tall, helped hang most of the wash. The ideal day for this would be sunny with a light breeze. The sun helped bleach the wash, and the breeze helped dry it. Temperature was not a big factor as long as the temperature was above freezing. Frozen laundry did not dry, and it did fray and crack.

After the laundry was dry, it was placed in the laundry basket, and taken to a table in the basement. Because we did not have a steam iron, the clothes were dampened using a water-filled catsup bottle with a sprinkler head attached to scatter droplets of water on each piece. The "sprinkled" cloth was then immediately rolled tight to keep and distribute its moisture until the ironing process began.

Meet My Waterloo   *Weekly Ritual*

During inclement weather and winter, the basement was used as the place for drying. Clothesline was strung in neat rows, and the laundry carefully hung starting at the most distant end from the washing process. Since neither a bleaching sun nor a drying breeze was present, complete drying was not required. Rather, the laundry was removed while still slightly damp, eliminating the "sprinkling" step. When laundry was drying in the basement, the humidity in the house would rise significantly, and, in winter, one could count on a thick layer of frost on the windows that Monday night.

Tuesday: Ironing Day
Few people know how many different irons exist. Most think of the electric steam irons used today. But we had irons of many types. There were two kinds of "flat irons." One was electric but without steam, and it was the primary instrument. The second type of flat iron was an implement made of solid iron (hence the name "iron"), the intent being to have sufficient mass to retain heat for a long period of time. These irons were used only to bridge the frequent power outages. Multiple irons of this type were placed on the stove so that they could alternately be heated and then used without interrupting the ironing progress.

Another form of iron was the "ruffle" iron. My grandmother's dressiest outfits included blouses with lacy ruffles at the collar, bib, and cuffs, and handkerchiefs always had a ruffle trim. Furthermore, any curtain worth hanging had a ruffle edge. A special iron was required for these adornments. The iron consisted of two pieces, one a flat plate with a corrugated or "gear-tooth" top, the other shaped like the bottom of a rocking chair with a corrugated bottom that meshed with the companion surface. These two segments were made of solid iron and heated on the stove. The iron was then placed on an insulated surface on the ironing board, the ruffled edge of the garment placed in between the two corrugated surfaces, and the top "rocked" to achieve the pressed, wavy presentation.

One day my father came home with his addition to the iron collection. He presented his labor-saving implement called a mangle. (What a name for a wrinkle remover!) It was a device much like the washer's wringer, but it was heated, making it highly useful for flat items such as sheets, pillow cases, towels, and handkerchiefs. But my grandmother was never satisfied with its "finish," so every piece processed by the mangle was given quick press on the top and bottom of the folded article with the hand iron lest the imperfect piece ever be seen by a visitor.

Two or three ironing boards were set up in the basement, and my grandmother and Barbara Mikenhiemner would iron away the day, dialoging in their Low Deutsche. My mother, too, was part of this team, listening and understanding the conversation, but responding only in English. She had left spoken German in her eighth grade classroom, and never spoke it again.

Wednesday and Thursday: Projects

Wednesdays and Thursdays were reserved for special tasks that needed to be accomplished. Tending the flowers and garden, picking fruit, canning, upholstering a chair, hanging screens or awnings, painting the porch swing, and the like, were tasks that would be allocated time during this mid-week span. In the summer, the lawn, which had to be perfectly groomed for the weekend, was religiously mowed on Wednesday so that the cuttings could be removed during the Thursday garbage pickup.

This was also a good time to "go quilting," a recreational and social event as well as a production effort. On one occasion, I was required to attend a quilting because my grandmother was my "baby sitter." I must confess that I did not understand one word spoken by the attendees except for those times when my grandmother specifically addressed me in English. These occasions were cherished opportunities for the participants to revert to their Low Deutsche, but I felt like I was trapped in a foreign country.

Friday: Baking and Shopping

Friday and Saturday were days used to prepare for the possibility of guests and visitors on Sunday. While relatives normally scheduled their visits in advance, drop-in friends were always welcome. Friday was dedicated to baking and shopping.

Baking was a joy for both my mother and grandmother. My grandmother made such delicacies as cherry, rhubarb, apple, and peach pies, baked apples, and stuffed tomatoes. My mother took her turn at cooking, showing her prowess with lemon meringue pies, and angel food and Devil's food cakes. Around Christmas, the two of them would collaborate on cookies, and every tin we owned would be filled. Friday was a good day for a kid to hang around the kitchen!

Friday was also "fast" day at our house. My grandmother, being Catholic, honored the Catholic protocol of avoiding "meat" on this day, and the rest of the family was given no choice. I never understood why she called it "fasting" though. Chappie, the great angler, usually delivered between twenty and thirty fresh fish weekly, and fish was not considered meat. My grandmother would fry the entire catch, and excepting the one fish my grandmother had, and one my mother forced herself to eat, we men devoured them all. (This is fasting?) Sunfish, crappie, blue gill, and bass are small, but we made up for that problem with quantity. And whatever secret recipe my grandmother used, it worked, because the fish were delicious. Once in a while, there was a catfish or two in the collection, and I loved them best of all because they were flavorful and fairly free of bones. Catfish were always mine.

Friday was also household shopping day for the few things you would purchase. I would be sent for Spotlight brand coffee, citrus fruit, and "greens" at Krogers, and meat products and baking supplies from Rau's. Friday was also payday for those households fortunate enough to have employment, and therefore, the stores remained open on Friday night until 9:00 P.M. to entice those with money to shop in exchange for cashing their checks. However, many of the taverns provided the same service, and it could get a little noisy on Friday night. I was sent on my missions in the afternoon.

Saturday: House Cleaning
Saturday was chores day. My mother and grandmother cleaned the house, changed all the bedding and linens, and made the home presentable for guests. Before I became a Saturday grocery boy, I would "sleep" in and listen to the sounds emanating from downstairs. My mother loved the music of an orchestra under the direction of Wayne King, and he had a Saturday morning radio program that she used as entertainment while she dusted, joining the music by humming. No vacuuming while this show was on! Following that show, my grandmother took over her rare control of the radio, and she listened to a program of singing canaries accompanied by an organ. How clever, I thought, that the sponsor was a bird seed company. No vacuuming during this program! But following these programs, the scream of the

Meet My Waterloo   *Weekly Ritual*

upright began, and my reverie would be shattered. Time to get up and get to work myself.

I was taught rather early in my childhood how to use an axe and hatchet, and cutting the kindling for the week was my job. This chore was conducted in the garage where wood was stored. The kindling was subsequently hauled into the basement. After completing this task, I would shovel the ashes from the "Monster" into buckets, and carry them to the ash pile at the rear of the property. Then, every piece of outdoor concrete would be swept (or shoveled if there was snow). This included the sidewalks, driveway, and front and rear porches, to make these approaches welcome for visitors. All these chores were the "regulars." I also served "at the pleasure" of my mother and grandmother for other tasks as they saw fit.

But if I had all my chores completed, Saturday afternoon was mine. I could always join a friend, and off we would go to the creek to play Cops-and-Robbers, to the farm for fun in the hayloft, to the mill pond to float a raft, to the train station to see the steam engines, or to the woods for Hide-and-Seek. There was no such place called a "playground" except for the one called *Waterloo*. "Be home by six" was the only admonition, "and don't forget, it's bath night!"

Sunday: Church and Company
Sunday was always special to everyone in the household, and each member had his or her own reason. For my grandmother, it was her day to get dressed in her finest to attend church and see her many friends. After that she could show off her prowess as a hostess if we had company. For my mother, church was also what made the day special. She too would dress in her finest, but for her the most important feature was that I was there at church with her. For my dad, Sunday

morning was time for horseshoes, cork ball, or kloeper (a card game). For Chappie, it was a morning to fish at Beaver Lake. For me, Sunday morning, with church and Sunday school, was more like school, and not something I looked forward to eagerly. But, if I willingly complied, I knew I would probably get a chance to go to the afternoon matinee at the Capitol Theatre, and *that* was special. Or, maybe Uncle Wilbur would be here, and that was even better.

Sunday morning, for me, would start with the beautiful sound of church bells. "Lloyd, time to get up and get ready for church" would float up the stairs from my mother. By nine-thirty, I was in Sunday School, and at eleven, in church service. Then home for dinner.

Sunday dinners were always made into an event. Even with "just family," a chicken dinner or roast would be served, not the usual weekly fare. But when guests came for dinner, that was even more special. Now the dining room table was set with the guest china and silverware, the linen tablecloth and napkins were brought out, and the napkins were placed in silver rings. Water goblets and miniature salt and pepper shakers graced each place, and cut glass relish trays and candle holders served each end of the table. Bread was placed on an oblong silver tray, gravy in the silver gravy boat, and even toothpicks appeared in their silver container.

Each attendee at the meal was dressed in "Sunday best". Of course, my grandmother, mother, and I were still in our "church" clothes. Chappie would go home after cleaning his fish in the back yard, and get dressed in his dress slacks, white shirt and tie. He would sport a straw hat, except at the table. Of course, any visitors were also appropriately dressed, as manners of the era dictated.

The food was "Sunday fare" and plenty of it. Fried chicken, mashed potatoes and gravy, green beans, stuffing, butter beans, stuffed tomatoes or baked apples, and stacks of bread circulated time and again around the festive table. The sumptuous meal was followed by pie baked on Friday, and coffee brewed in the silver electric percolator.

On many occasions, Wilbur would join us for the weekend, and, of course, the Sunday dinner. How I loved it when he came; it usually meant an afternoon exploring expedition or a fishing trip to Beaver Lake. And Sunday dinner was always more entertaining when he was present because of the lively conversation he stimulated around the table. My dad and Chappie usually had similar views on various subjects because they both lived in Waterloo, but Wilbur, being an "out-of-towner," often had another perspective. Even if he secretly agreed with them, he would bait them with a counter-argument just for the stimulation. How angry Chappie could get: "Aw, you just don't know what you're talking about," he would declare in disgust. But rough edges were usually smoothed over after dinner with a glass of wine or beer.

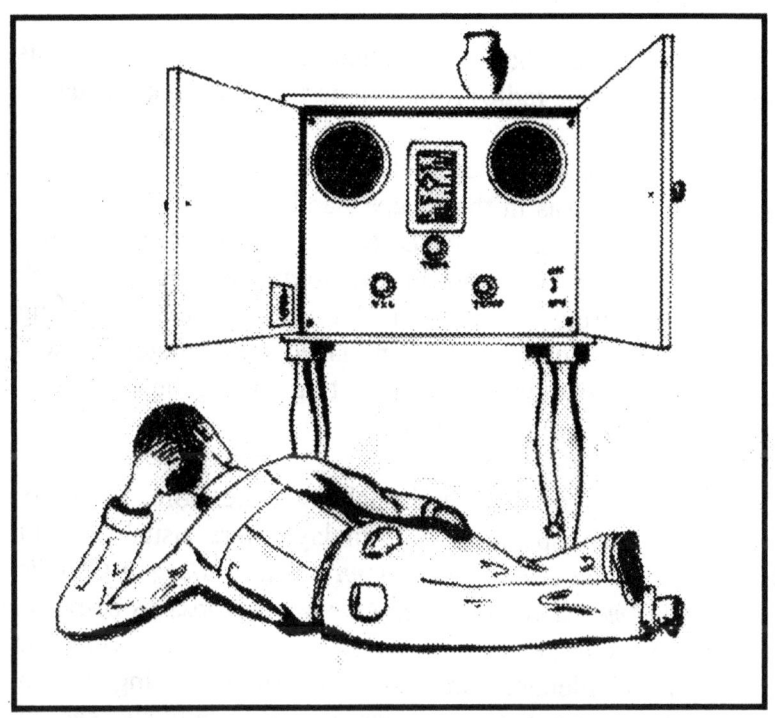

Listening to the Radio

Chapter 16   Radio

The cherry tree, the attic, and the shed all enhanced my adventure world, and that world was of my design and direction. The fantasy or experiment was given direction by me -- I could style and vary the outcome any way I pleased. But radio was different. Here I was a captive to the program's story and I had to tag along. And the mystery of the unknown outcome was exhilarating. Radio stimulated the imagination as much as, or even more than your free-form fantasies. You could imagine the open range for the *Lone Ranger* show, picture a foreboding mansion during *Inner Sanctum*, or descend a guarded stairway to Jack Benny's basement vault.

The set could be what you wanted, but not the story. This marvelous box (the radio) formed a part of our weekly ritual.

The role radio played in each of our lives varied. My mother's primary interest was in the "soaps," and the radio was hers on weekday afternoons. *Valiant Lady* was escape from her humdrum captivity in a mother-in-law dominated routine. Work did not stop during the program. Rather, work such as ironing or sewing that could be accomplished while listening was selected on weekdays, as was dusting during her Saturday morning *Wayne King* show.

My father loved comedy and challenge; therefore, the early evening hours (especially on Sunday) were usually spent listening to *Fred Allan, Jack Benny, Edgar Bergen-Charlie McCarthy, Amos and Andy,* and *Our Miss Brooks* as comedy, and the *Sixty-Four Dollar Question* and *Quiz Kids* for intellectual challenge. An aspect of programming which astounded him was that a ventriloquist show could succeed on radio. But the reasons were really clear. You imagined the ventriloquist's dummy in action, and heard the live audience respond with laughter, all of which provided validity that it was indeed happening. More important, the show was a well written comedy that did not need Charlie McCarthy to be a dummy in order to be funny.

Some shows suited the whole family's tastes, and it was common for us to listen to the *Lux Radio Theater* and *Major Bowes' Amateur Hour* together. The Lux show was especially intriguing because it produced radio versions of movies that had been released in the past, and one had a chance to relive the movie without having to watch a screen or leave home. Some of the shows even used the same stars on radio that had performed the roles in the movie.

Meet My Waterloo   <u>Radio</u>

My grandmother did not have a large interest in radio. She would listen to the "soaps" and family programs, but she would not initiate the activity. When I was quite young, my grandmother had a canary whose cage hung in the kitchen. Saturday morning, she would tune to the program of singing canaries accompanied by an organ, but I believe that selection was more for the well being of the canary than for her own.

For me, the radio was another dimension of adventure. There were a few daily episodes produced specifically for children. These programs would air before supper, and each was fifteen minutes in length. You had to be selective in your listening, because there were multiple radio stations vying for your attention, and your interest in Wheaties or Ovaltine or Wonder Bread. This gave you the choice of *Tom Mix*, *Lone Ranger* (and Tonto), *Red Ryder* (and Little Beaver), *Sky King*, *Jack Armstrong*, the *Shadow*, the *Green Hornet*, *Superman*, and more, with an imaginary setting for each show and episode.

When I was very young, around Christmas time, there was a fifteen minute "Santa Claus" show during which time the names of "good" and "need improvement" children were read. Elation if you ever heard your name on the "good" list, but real worry when it appeared on the "bad." And you had to listen every night, because your name came up only once a season!

After supper, I was required to work on my homework. Several programs were allowed during the week as a reward if my grades were good, and my homework for the next day completed. My favorite two programs were the *Inner Sanctum*, and *Suspense*. Each program was designed to present frightening situations, and their descriptive power to

Meet My Waterloo   *Radio*

stimulate the imagination was outstanding. When the program setting was in a dark, eerie forest, you were suddenly in a dark, eerie forest, not your own safe home. And then you were in as much danger as the program's main character. Having been exposed to certain movies did not help either. If the story line described some sinister work in a laboratory, you could easily conjure up Frankenstein's cellar. A scene with dark woods refreshed your memory of the Wolf Man hiding behind a tree. At least with the movies you were safe when you got home, but with radio, the danger came right into your living room!

Radios were a luxury in many households during the 1930s. Fortunately, we had a small radio that was acquired in Chicago, and it lasted throughout my childhood. That radio sat on a tiny corner table in the kitchen because that room was our main living space. Around 1940, we acquired another radio, this one a "console" model designed as a piece of furniture. It looked like a combination end table and knick-knack table and stood on four decorative legs. It was fun to lie in front of this radio in the living room, in the dark, and listen to the adventure programs. Since no one else enjoyed these shows, I had the adventure room all to myself.

Radio fell into the weekly pattern of living. Sunday night was dedicated to such programs as *Quiz Kids, Jack Benny, Fred Allan, Charlie McCarthy, Our Miss Brooks, Gene Autry* (mostly singing), and the *Sixty-Four Dollar Question*. Monday night we listened to *Lux Radio Theater*; Tuesday night, *Inner Sanctum*; Wednesday night, *Major Bowes*; Thursday night, *Suspense*; Saturday morning, *Wayne King* and the canaries (that's not a rock group); and Saturday night, the *Lucky Strike Hit Parade*. I miss them all!

The Drum Major

Chapter 17   Tradition

The Drum Major
The municipal band not only played the weekly concerts, but also marched in many of the parades sponsored by Waterloo and its surrounding communities. For these occasions, the band had elegant maroon uniforms, and wearing them in a parade representing Waterloo was a proud occasion. Otis Lutz normally played in the band (a clarinet player, I've been told), however, when the band participated in the parades, Otis became the drum major. Not only could he strut as if this were the only band in the world, but he could do it in his own personal style. How anyone could walk leaning so far back

was beyond my comprehension. By the laws of physics, he should have crashed to the ground on his back, but yet, here was this gregarious leader of the band proudly marching in front as if this were the most important moment of his life. I remember with the greatest fondness that happy, ear-to-ear smile telling everyone that he was proud of this band.

Nicknames and Baseball

Nicknames were prevalent in Waterloo during my parents' generation, and almost every male in the town had one. (The tradition was somewhat diminished by my time, but we still had "Bussy," "Lu Lu," "Toots," "Auts," "Hoppy," and "Pete.") My uncle's alias was "Cocky," and with good reason. He was the catcher for an independent baseball team, and it did not pay to challenge him at home plate.

Every town had several baseball teams. The competition was fierce, and rivalries were intense. All the players could be good friends off the field, but on the field, it was war. The game was not only "high spikes," but psychological as well. The Waterloo team on which Wilbur played had two brothers, the Erds, who were pitchers. Both brothers had the disabilities of being unable to hear or speak, and therefore, they spoke to each other in sign language. Wilbur also knew sign language, and, from his catcher's position he would communicate the pitching strategy that way. There were times when the pitcher and catcher would just have a long "conversation" and then, on cue, both break out laughing. Of course, the batter thought they were ridiculing him and would become angry. But angry batters usually did not hit well. This tactic was reserved for critical situations with several opponents on base, two outs, and the game's score close in the late innings. The batter would become even more furious as he struck out, but you didn't take out your frustration on "Cocky." How Wilbur laughed after the game: "We got another one!"

Thanksgiving
My dad and uncle traditionally went rabbit hunting on Thanksgiving Day. They had a standing invitation at Billy's (he was a local farmer), and would hunt until they had the limit, or Billy called them in. Life on the farm did not bring many opportunities for socializing, and therefore Billy welcomed these two visitors on this special occasion so he could have companions for a pinochle game and some "refreshment." Later in the day, Dad and Wilbur would return home, dress the rabbits, and get cleaned up for supper. How I loved to see the rabbits; it signaled a change in menu for the coming Sunday.

During the day, my mother and grandmother would start preparations for the Thanksgiving meal, the only "special occasion" meal served at supper time. This meal always included the classic turkey and all the trimmings. Wilbur would bring me something to work on while the hunting was taking place, and the surprise might be sketch books, coloring books, or "Big Little" adventure books. I would sit in the kitchen engrossed in my project, inhaling the good smells of supper in preparation. I was even allowed to be the judge of the stuffing flavor (always suggesting "more sage"), and was permitted to enjoy the "odds and ends" treats, such as the turkey neck and liver. Also, I especially had to check out the pumpkin pie.

Dinner itself was served in the kitchen since there were no guests (Wilbur was family, not a guest even though he lived in St. Louis). With six people at the table, and the turkey platter in the middle, most of the remaining food had to be placed on the sideboard until it was time for that dish to circulate. My grandmother ferried the food between the sideboard and table ensuring everyone was served. Between the delicious supper and the afternoon "refreshments" by the hunters, this was one of the more jovial meals of the year. And there were always plenty of leftovers!

<u>Christmas</u>
The entire family collaborated to make my Christmas a delightful one. Tradition in our household dictated that the tree, decorations, and presents would all be delivered by Santa on Christmas Eve, and the gifts would be opened that evening. And how I hated to go to that *darn* Christmas program at church where I had to perform when all the exciting action was at home!

My mother's role was to get me away from the house which she did by accompanying me to church, and to *keep* me away until all of the decorating was completed at home by my dad and grandmother. Therefore, as soon as the church service was over, my mother would decide that she wanted to see the town's decorations. We would drive from street to street while she enthusiastically pointed to one beautiful display after another. And I could not have cared less. I wanted to go home and open the presents I KNEW were there. Finally, we would drive by my house, and sometimes end the tour, but just as often, to make matters even worse, Mother would decide there was another street or two to check out. Little did I know that the upstairs window shade was the local semaphore. Up, "It's okay to bring him home," down, "We're not ready yet!"

While I was away, Dad would mount the tree in its stand, place the stand in the middle of an electric train set, and then string the lights. My grandmother would follow him around the tree attaching ornaments on the branches. When those tasks were finished, both of them would hang "icicles" on the tree, although, to hear my grandmother, Dad just *threw* them at the tree. Packages were retrieved from secret places (from under my grandmother's bed, I later found out), and placed around the tree. The decorations were not complete until the candy jar was filled, cookies were distributed on snack plates, mistletoe was hung from lamps, pine cones were placed on the bookcase, and ribbons were tied to anything upright. The train was started, and the window shade could go up!

When my mother finally released me from my automotive prison, I would rush to the door. Even outside I could hear the train making its circular route around the tree. "Santa's been here!" I would be corralled long enough to remove my coat, cap and gloves, and then receive that joyous release, "Go to it!"

The presents included a judicious mix of toys and clothes, The toys were usually from my list prepared before Christmas. (A few weeks before Christmas, my mother would suggest that Santa would appreciate any help I could give by checking a FEW items in the toy catalog.) Clothes were usually replacements for tattered predecessors but of a more appropriate size. Of course, everyone else was also opening presents, including the hand-made offerings from me that I had secretly given my grandmother to place under the tree for me. I can still see the smiles of my family enjoying me.

By this time it was late. The church service had ended at 9:00 P.M., and the town tour, around 10:00 P.M., the present opening, around 11:00 P.M., or later. As much as I wanted to play with my toys now, it was almost impossible to stay awake. Although I was reluctant to quit, sleep did seem to be a good idea. "Tomorrow is another day." And you can bet I did not sleep in.

Part VI
Fun

Chapter 18   **Swimming**

Chapter 19   **The Field**

Chapter 20   **Games and Other Delights**

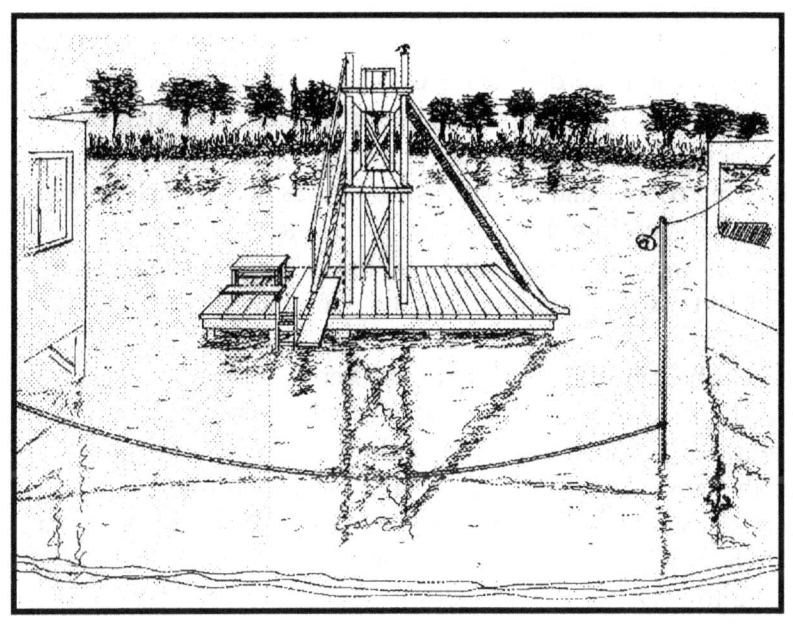

The Raft

Chapter 18   Swimming

Summer in Illinois is both hot and humid, an uncomfortable pairing of conditions. To combat the sticky heat of the afternoon, you closed the house, pulled down the shades, and, on very bad days, spent time in the basement. Closing the house kept the hot outside air from convecting in. The drawn shades reflected some of the heat, and our retreat to the basement counted on the latent cooling of the thick concrete walls and floor. Poor adults! We kids cooled off by swimming.

The first swimming activity that I remember took place at the public facility on North Market Street. It was small, about double the size of a modern home pool. Steps led into the shallow end, and the depth increased to about eight feet at the far end. The deep end had a wooden platform for sunbathing and "hanging out." The pool was surrounded by bushes, but, to the best of my recollection, it had no protective fence, no dressing rooms, and no bathrooms. It was heavily chlorinated, and was therefore a significant irritant to your eyes. Since I did not know how to swim, I willingly stayed at the shallow end, and played under the watchful eye of my mother.

Creeks became the next source of afternoon revitalization. The tree-lined Koenigsmark Creek ran near our house, and was a natural playground for some children. While the depth of most of the creek was only a few inches, shallows were formed by blocked water flow, and some of these were a foot or two in depth. While not useful for swimming, it was a refreshing place to play. Shoes and clothes were left on the bank, and a splashing good time was had by all.

Fountain Creek provided a more adventurous swimming hole after we were old enough to have bicycles. One such location was about a half-mile south of the Water Works on the Maeystown Road. The creek here had several "holes" that were deeper than we were tall, and had high banks along the sides from which we could jump. A vine had been pulled loose from an overhanging tree so we could "Tarzan" into the creek for even more excitement.

Fountain Creek sites were "unsanctioned" since we had to ride our bikes some distance out of town and there was, of course, no lifeguard. Both activities were considered unsupervised. Therefore, you did not announce your intentions for this swimming. You had to be sure not to get your clothes wet, for wet clothes were a clear clue to your activity. Fortunately, your hair would dry on the bike ride home. Since the creek was partially shaded by the surrounding woods, the tanning effect of the sun was slowed, and we were clever enough to ensure we were uniformly tanned all over. But after a few weeks, it was impossible to hide the deep tan. My explanations were received with skepticism.

Once we tried swimming in the Mississippi River near Valmeyer, but one attempt taught us all the lessons we needed: *avoid this river!* The Illinois River flows through three hundred miles of farmland, the Mississippi to the north, through eight hundred miles of prairie, and the Missouri to the west, through fifteen hundred miles of Great Plains. All three rivers converge about fifty miles north of Valmeyer and homogenize their residue into one soupy mud flow. We could not see anything in the water. The river had a significant amount of debris that hurt when it hit you. Eddies swirled near the shoreline and, if they were not pulling you under, they would spin you into disorientation. We were surprised at our level of disappointment and amazed at the danger in swimming in this water -- it was not the romantic adventure of Huck or Tom. We sensibly stayed away after that.

The swimming location that most of my generation will remember is the lake at the Waterloo Country Club. For twenty-five cents, you could swim in the lake. The immediate shore line between the clubhouse and boathouse had a gravel beach and a shallow roped-off area for the younger or inexperienced aquanaut. Farther out in the lake, a recreational structure had been built in about twelve feet of water. It had a diving board and two diving platforms, one at three meters height, the second, at eight meters. The lower level was accessed by ladder, the upper, by a steep stairway. A slide was attached to the upper platform and provided a thrilling glide from the top to the water's surface.

Meet My Waterloo   *Swimming*

A swimmer was required to stay within the shallow roped-off area of the lake until you could prove that your swimming skills were sufficiently developed to access the "raft" (as the platform was erroneously known). Proof of your ability was demonstrated to the lifeguard by swimming the length of the restraining rope secured at one end to a lamppost, and at the other to the boathouse. On the first swim to the raft after a successful demonstration, the lifeguard accompanied the swimmer for his initiation trip. After that, you were free to enjoy the summer recreation on your own.

One had to follow certain rules concerning activities on the raft. Rule One, no running. Rule Two, only one person on the slide at a time. Rule Three, only one person on the diving board at a time. These rules were easy enough to follow until you engaged in a game of Tag. Now we would race up the stairs and leap or dive from the top platform, or, under certain conditions, sail down the slide to avoid being tagged by the person who was "it." This activity was permitted until it was obvious it was getting dangerous, at which time we suffered "penalty time," ten minutes just sitting, fifteen minutes in the shallow part of the lake, or a half-hour out of the lake, the choice of penalty dependent on the degree of our misbehavior.

The slide was an attractive feature of the raft. Unfortunately, when the structure was built, the slide was placed on the south side of the raft, receiving the full burden of the afternoon sun. The slide was made of stainless steel, and would heat to a sufficiently high temperature to injure one's skin. Therefore, a hand pump was installed on the top platform to permit the use of lake water to cool the slide and provide a slippery surface. While great for casual recreation, the slide was useless as a Tag escape route unless you were absolutely sure someone had very recently bathed the incline with cooling water.

Meet My Waterloo — Swimming

The Country Club facilities were operated by Bill Lieb. He managed the restaurant and bar, took care of the daily swimming and golf registrations, and kept an eye out on our deportment (over and above the watchful eye of the lifeguard). He enjoyed having a safe place for the kids to play, and made you feel welcome. But he did rule with a firm hand. He had a strong sense of safety.

In the winter, the lake would occasionally freeze over. Then, you could spend your quarter skating, but only after Bill made sure (in his own style) the ice was safe. He would drive a tractor onto the surface, and comment "If it doesn't fall in, you can skate!" He would deliberately frustrate us all in answering the question we asked, "What will you do if it *does* fall in?" thinking primarily of *his* safety. All we ever got was a grin, and, "Well, then, it's not safe for skating." We never had to worry.

The Field

Chapter 19   The Field

Small Midwest towns usually have intimate contact with farms at their periphery. But for Waterloo, and especially near my home, the farmland intruded far inside the town boundaries, creating a huge field as a continuation of my backyard. This proximity allowed me to witness the farming routine. Winter wheat, planted in the fall, could be harvested in late spring, permitting a second crop to mature by fall. Corn, planted early in the spring would be harvested in August or September, with the corn stacks in place for Halloween. Oats occasionally replaced wheat, and alfalfa or clover cycled through the sequence for soil restoration as well as cattle feed. Typically, the land would lie fallow during the winter, and be blanketed with tall grasses, making it possible to hunt rabbits seeking cover in this growth.

Meet My Waterloo   *The Field*

Hunting within the town boundaries! And it was safe, because there were no homes between Main Street and Moore Street in the east-west direction, and none between the Koenigsmark Creek and northern town boundary of Columbia Avenue in the north-south direction. The only land features in this entire area were the hedge row dividing the plot into two fields, and a statuesque black walnut tree standing guard somewhat near the middle of the acreage. A drainage slope carved by decades of runoff from the summer rains funneled water towards Koenigsmark Creek. Because of the slopes, plowing across the face of the runoff was undertaken to prevent erosion. A small boy could learn such information by offering a cup of cool cistern water to the sweating farmer who was happy to relate what he was doing in between gulps. Of course, I was looking for a ride on the big iron wheeled tractor, but farmers were all business. There was no recreation while there was work to be done.

The adults had mixed feeling about this field being located within the town. Their primary concern was the insect infestation that accompanied each crop's maturing. Corn brought the grasshoppers, and my grandmother would be furious if her flowers or vegetable garden were attacked. The grasshoppers forced many an early harvest for her garden. On the other hand, alfalfa brought the bees that pollinated the plants rather than harming them (or you as long as you did not disturb them). Wheat had bugs, but these insects were not as invasive as oat bugs. Oat bugs were sufficiently small that they could penetrate ordinary screens. And they could both bite and cause itching! You could not escape their presence by remaining in the house. Because most houses had no air conditioning, you had to open the windows to receive the cooling evening breeze, and then the oat bug attack was on.

Meet My Waterloo   *The Field*

The field became an extension of my play area at certain times of the year. After a crop was harvested, only stubble would remain and it was acceptable to play on this surface. It was an especially great place to fly a kite since there were no telephone poles or wires to interfere, and no trees, save the stately black walnut.

To be a real kite flyer, you had to make your own kite. Two strips (for a "two sticker") or three strips ("three sticker") of thin pine or fir were symmetrically crossed and nailed together at their intersection. String was fastened around the periphery and held in place by notches cut at the end of the sticks. To this framework, newspaper was attached as the plane surface, using flour paste as glue. Attach a rag tail to the back, a bow line across the face, your kite string to the bow line, and you were ready to fly! Tailoring the tail length to wind conditions was part of the learning process. Accepting the consequences of rapid wind changes was too.

The challenge in kite flying is to see what height you can achieve. When successful, you had to pay out a large amount of string. If the wind died rapidly, you had to be adept at reeling the string back in because the kite could not support the joint weight of the string and heavy tail without a strong wind. It was then that you found out that the black walnut tree and your kite were oppositely polarized so the solitary growth inevitably captured your kite. And the kite would hang in its Purgatory for months, visible as it whirled in the cold winter wind. Since the walnut tree knew it was viewable from our house, its deliberate taunting of me was undeniable!

There were other reasons to dislike black walnut trees. Not that their nuts weren't delicious, for they were, especially on

Christmas cookies. But I remain convinced that the black walnut was named not for the color of the nut, but the color you turned trying to get the nut. Each nut shell was surrounded by a green casing. The pods were left to dry and then removed to expose the shell. But the green pod was black on the inside, and a tar-like substance appeared on both the pod interior, and shell exterior. If you touched either, the material could stain your skin, and it would take months for the stain to disappear. Nonetheless, we made annual trips to the tree to gather the nuts for baking later in the season.

After the harvesting of wheat or oats, the stalk of the plant was left on the ground by the reaper. Later, when dry, these stalks were gathered as hay for livestock. This process used a hay baler drawn by a tractor to "sweep" up the straw from the ground, and force the straw into a packing chute. When the chute was full, wires were placed around the packed material to retain its shape. This hay bale was then dumped on the ground, and the process repeated until all the hay had been baled. The scattered hay bales were then picked up by truck or horse-drawn hay wagon and taken to another part of the field where they were neatly stacked.

From my back yard, this stack of hay bales looked like a rectangular stone fortress. As soon as the workers left the field, we would race to the stack and climb up. In a matter of days, we would rearrange the top layers of the bales to have tunnels and a secret clubhouse, none of which were viewable from the ground. We could retain this private world until the farmers retrieved the hay for their farms and wintertime livestock feeding.

It was always fun to have corn be the crop of the year. After the corn reached a height of about three feet, you could play

Meet My Waterloo   *The Field*

between the rows without damaging the crop, and therefore an expanded play yard was available. When the corn reached maturity however, it was so much taller than we were, that it was no longer fun to play among the rows. In fact, the tall stalks damped your sound, and covered it with a wind driven rustle of their own. You could neither see nor hear your companion in play.

But, when the corn was harvested, the corn stalks would be cut and arranged in stacks we called "shocks." These became excellent hiding places for Hide-and-Seek. We also played Cops-and-Robbers with cap guns, but almost without fail, our cap guns would be banned lest a spark ignite the shocks.

It is now evident that the field was destined to be a playground for children. Perhaps we even paved the way, for today, that field has been leveled and converted to a playground for children and a baseball field for young athletes. I like to think we taught the field to love children!

Third Street Sledding

Chapter 20   Games And Other Delights

The nature of our recreation changed as a function of our maturity, the status of the Depression and war, and the seasons. In the early grades, our recreation centered around the inflated rubber ball, usually supplied by our school. Oh, the games one could conjure up using that ball! One such game was Kickball, a variation of baseball. The ball was rolled from the pitcher's "mound" to home plate. You used your foot to kick the ball instead of a bat to hit it, but the remainder of the game was played by the rules of baseball (except that sometimes we played "one bounce is out"). Any number could play because all the "extras" went into the outfield.

Another ball-oriented game was high energy Keep-Away. Again, any number could play. Teams were chosen by every means conceivable. Sometimes two popular classmates were selected as captains who alternately selected teammates. Sometimes it was "boys against the girls," and sometimes a couple of "meanies" (also the best athletes) would mischievously agree to try to keep the ball away from everyone else. Boys versus the girls was not too widely accepted by the boys, since, at this stage of our development, some of the girls were better athletes.

And what a high energy game Keep-Away was! You ran at full speed all the time, yelling and shouting instructions or encouragement every second. Obesity was not a problem known to us. The game was so engrossing and noisy that on one occasion, not one player heard the bell ring an end to recess, and we continued to play until minutes later, someone noticed we were the only grade still on the playground. While we were subsequently "grounded" for a few recess periods, the principal reason for the punishment was a show of discipline enforcement to other classes. The teacher knew that, in our exuberance, we just did not hear the bell!

The rubber ball could be used for any game requiring an object to be carried, thrown, hit, or kicked, and therefore, games were developed resembling baseball (Kickball), football, and soccer (Keep-Away and Dodge-'Em). Each class at the public school had such a rubber ball for physical education class, and it was loaned out for recess. But we also knew how to have fun without "purchased" props. This was especially true when you were not under "school time." Tag, Hide-and-Seek, Crack-the-Whip, and Red Rover required no props at all. Kick-the-Can required only a tin can be added to the activity and you had a game that involved hiding, seeking, racing, and kicking. These games, of course, were devised to suit the times in which there was no money for "toys." Our

Meet My Waterloo *Games And Other Delights*

imaginations devised props when necessary from available "stuff."

As we grew older, some refinements were made in the games. Kickball gave way to softball. While you needed one bat and one ball, no fielders' gloves were necessary. Softball eventually surrendered to baseball when a fielder's glove became the object of each boy's birthday or Christmas wish. For football, the round inflated rubber ball was difficult to carry and impossible to accurately or strategically pass, therefore, the availability of a real football allowed Touch, a game with the scoring rules of football, but played without the expensive protective padding and uniforms. Touch was played both with and without school supervision. But when we had an excess of energy and no adults were watching, we played Tackle, and what bruises we incurred without that protective padding! I joined such a game after violin practice. (My father attempted violin in his youth, and I was given an equal opportunity at suffering with his violin). I placed the instrument along the sideline and play began. On one particular "end run," I raced along the sideline as the ball carrier until blasted out of bounds by the opposition, and I landed on the violin case. Not only was I bruised, but I also had a box of kindling to explain to my parents.

Not all our recreation involved a scoring incentive. Some was just for pure enjoyment of activity. Bicycling, ice skating, and sledding provided some of our pleasures as well, but these activities required that you own personal athletic equipment. My grandfather was foresighted enough to save his children's sled, and he kept it in good shape for his grandson, me. The sled hung in the basement, and it was declared mine, probably the minute I was born. Ice skates also were "inherited." I found a pair of shoe skates in an attic storage trunk. These had belonged to my uncle, but no longer fit him. Because of their age, the leather was in poor shape, but I did manage to get some skating accomplished on these blades during the brief period when their size was appropriate for me. The bicycle was also a gift from my uncle Wilbur. He loved bicycling, and rode his bike to work in St. Louis for a time. But when his commute became too lengthy, and the traffic too dangerous, he no longer could use the bike and gave it to me.

Ice skating depended on having a suitable lake or pond, and this activity took place at either the Country Club (supervised) or Mill Pond (unsupervised). The Mill Pond was within walking distance, averaged only a few feet deep (therefore it was safe), and had a sufficiently broad shore that you could build a bonfire to warm up, or roast marshmallows. We would skate there even when we had not experienced the week of sub-zero nights to generate thick ice. There was the possibility of falling through thin ice and getting wet up to your waist, but this meant no worse of an outcome than catching a cold.

Bicycling was not thought of as a recreational activity (even though we knew plenty of ways to enjoy this vehicle), but rather, as a means of transportation. But sledding was something different; the sled came out only on the few occasions you had six or more inches of snow, and it was not transportation, it was fun.

On the occasion of a deep snow, Third Street was dedicated to the children, and was not cleared. This thoroughfare was a steep hill with the crest at Main Street, and the bottom five blocks below just past Moore Street. All side streets along that route were blocked to car traffic and one could sled in safety from cross traffic. A running start and a belly flop onto your sled at Rex's on Main Street and away you went, down this steep hill, gathering speed along the way past Church Street, then Library, then Salsbury, then Rau, and finally, Moore Street. Moore Street had a slight elevation (crown) that started the slow-down process. Third Street was flat after that, and the sled gradually slowed. The challenge was to see if you could coast all the way to the power plant. It was a long walk back up the hill, but the ride down was worth the climb.

Of course, we invented ways to make it more fun, if not somewhat hazardous. Two or three could gang up on one sled in bobsled fashion, and get more speed because of the increased pressure on the runners. Four to a sled was even more fun, but rarely succeeded all the way down the hill. To get four on the sled, you had to lie down and kids were stacked on top of one another in a vertical pile. Three would get on the sled, and the fourth, would start the mass down the hill by pushing. Then at the right moment, the pusher would leap on top of the stack as the fourth rider. This arrangement raised the center of gravity fairly high, and any inaccuracy in the top person's placement toppled the ride before it really got started in earnest. Also, any sharp turn by the squashed driver on the bottom of the stack would cause bodies to sail off the sled sideways in a heap of snow and laughter.

To warm up, one would go into Rex's Confectionery. The warmth of the room and press of friends removed the outside chill, and soon had you back in the spirit of sledding.

Part VII
Adventure

Chapter 21   Trains

Chapter 22   Airplanes

The Train's Water Stop

Chapter 21   Trains

The Water Stop

"WHOOOOOOOOOOOOOO, WHOOOOOOOOOOOOOO, TOOT, WHOOOOOOOOOOOOOO!"

The train, pulled by a steam locomotive, was approaching the county road HH crossing screaming its two longs, a short, and a long signal from the steam powered horn. The signal was a warning that an unstoppable machine was going to roar through the intersection. On warm summer nights, I would lie on my bed by the open attic window and listen to the distant sound of the huffing locomotive. In the winter, the cold and dense air conducted the sound much better, but now the window, closed by necessity against the frozen air, damped the sound.

Meet My Waterloo   *Trains*

---- **SHUSH SHUSH SHUSH SHUSH SHUSH SHUSH SHUSH**-------. Each stroke of the piston powering the drive wheels of the locomotive produced a "shush," and these staccato releases of steam let me know that the train was still moving at high speed as it raced towards town. Then you could feel the engineer move the throttle forward as the frequency of the shushes was reduced, becoming slower and slower as the train sidled up to the town, stopping with a final **HISSSSSSSSSSSS.** Time to recharge!

The railroad tracks lay on the western edge of Waterloo, and most businesses associated with the railroad service were situated nearby. The milk company, the power plant, the two grain mills, the coal yards, and the train station were strung out along the main tracks and siding. Adjacent to the railroad station was a tall wooden water tank elevated by large timbers. To get high efficiency from the steam locomotives, the pressure released on each piston stroke also expelled steam, causing a significant loss of water. At strategically located towns therefore, water towers were erected to permit recharging the locomotives' water supply. A locomotive would position itself just past the tower's retractable arm so that water could be loaded into the tender, a companion rail car directly behind the locomotive. The tender's function was to carry the coal and water needed to power the locomotive.

It was easy for me to visualize each of the steps of the recharging process by listening to the sounds that emanated from the depot. First, **HISSSSSSS,** the final hiss of released steam as the locomotive stopped. Then, **CLANK,** the tender's water tank lid opening, **ARRONCONCH,** the squeak of the counterweighted tower spigot being lowered, **SHSHSHSH-SHSHSHSHSHSHSHSHSH,** the rush of the water flowing

Meet My Waterloo   *Trains*

from the tower into the tender, **THUMP,** the thud of the spigot being raised against the tower, **BANG!**, the crash of the tender's door being closed, and the warning **"TOOT TOOT,"** two short bursts of the steam whistle warning the brakeman and the switchman that the train was ready to roll.

Illinois is fairly flat country, ideal for farming and railroading. Therefore, a single locomotive could move a very long, heavily laden train since it would encounter very little grade change during its journey. Only one problem! The locomotive had to first get the train moving! Each car of a freight train provides some resistance to movement in the form of its weight (mass) and axle friction. The longer the train, the greater the resistance to moving. The locomotive's ability to get the train moving depends a great deal on its own weight as well as its power. As the locomotive applies its power, its wheels push backwards against the track, and the wheels keep from slipping only because of the friction proportional to the locomotive's weight. I could hear the first release of steam to the drive piston -- **HUSSH** -- meaning that the locomotive was attempting to move forward. Alas, the locomotive frequently encountered an excessive load (a load greater than its weight and friction could support), and its wheels would slip, wildly expending energy without rolling. The initial "hush" would be followed by staccato blasts of steam -- **CH CH CH CH CH CH CH CH CH** -- and I could clearly visualize the engineer lunging forward on the throttle lever to stop the attempt at acceleration. Next the engineer would release a little sand under each drive wheel in an attempt to get better traction. **HUSSH** -- and then -- **CH CH CH CH CH CH CH CH** -- the load was still too great.

Now we will see how smart the engineer was. When the train stopped to refuel, each car of the train applied its own brakes to help stop the train. Between every car there is a coupler that connects the cars together. Each coupler has some spare space as manufacturing tolerance and alignment error for the train; as much as one-half inch of spare space per coupler can exist. Over the length of a one-hundred-car train, the accumulated spare space is about four feet. Because each car helped stop the train, all the spare space was used up stretching the train to its full length. Therefore, when the locomotive attempted to get the train moving, it was, in fact, trying to move the heavy load of all the cars at once.

But the engineer had a way of overcoming the problem. His first act was to change the direction lever from the "forward" to the "reverse" position. Then, he slowly pulled the throttle to move the locomotive. As it inched backwards, the only load was the locomotive until the slack between the tender and the first boxcar was consumed. **CLUNK.** Then the locomotive, tender, and first boxcar moved back to use up the space between the first and second car, **CLUNK** each sequence taking up the slack space and adding to the mass of the front of the train and helping move each succeeding portion of the train. **BANK----CLANK-----CLUNK------BANG-----BANG CLANK** as the couplers gave up their spare space until the train was "compressed." But now the engineer reversed the momentum. After moving the lever from "reverse" to "forward," he advanced the throttle. Again, the first movement was solely that of the locomotive and tender until the spare space between the tender and first car was retrieved -- **CLANK!** Now the locomotive, tender, and first car rolled forward alone until the next coupler's spare space was extended -- **CLUNK!** And so it went, as each car added to the chain contributed mass to help move the remaining train.

Meet My Waterloo — Trains

There was a radical difference in sound that resulted from the forward motion as opposed to the backward motion of this activity. When the engineer put the train into reverse, he would just inch the locomotive backwards, slowly using up the coupler's spare space. The process was so slow that there was an adequate interval between "clunks" to count the cars. His intent was to use up the spare space, not to have the train highly energized in the reverse direction. However, when it was time to move the train forward, his action was much different. Now he plied the forward power with all the energy he could muster from the locomotive to get one huge surge. As a result all the slack space was given up in a matter of a second. **CLANKCLANKCLANKCLANKCLANKCLANK -- CLANK!** The staccato clanking of the couplers was dramatic and loud. Many a night I would awaken at the crash of that sound, and then be aware that the engine was successfully moving the train **HUSH---------------HUSH-------HUSH---HUSH--HUSH--**. Minutes later, I would hear the signal as the engineer approached Amrine's crossing:

"WHOOOOOOOOOOOOOO,
WHOOOOOOOOOOOOOO,
TOOT,
WHOOOOOOOOOOOOOO."

The Siding

For most of its route, the railroad used a single track for its traffic. Trains traveling in opposite directions, or trains traveling the same direction but at different speeds, had to be timed and coordinated so that one train would be on a second, parallel track (called a siding) while the other train passed by. These sidings were almost always located at a town that had a station master who could communicate by telegraph with

Meet My Waterloo   *Trains*

neighboring stations, and could give directions to the arriving trains by semaphore and signal lights.

Waterloo had such a siding, and, in fact, multiple sidings, one paralleling the through track, others curving away to facilitate freight car delivery to the industries that were dependent on railroad transportation. These freight cars might be loaded with sacks of flour from the Koenigsmark Mill, with corn from the Horn Mill, or with milk containers from the Waterloo Milk Company. Coal, lumber, heavy equipment and the like were also delivered for use by the community.

The train usually fell into one of three categories -- the long-haul freighter, a switcher, or the "milk run." Each type used the tracks in a different way. The long-haul freighters were primarily interested in delivering specified boxcars to the town, and picking up designated cars for delivery elsewhere. These trains usually left the cars it delivered on a siding, without distributing them to the local businesses. Similarly, the cars intended for them to pick up would be pre-assembled for them on the siding. The train would deliver new cars, pick up waiting cars, take on water if necessary, and leave as rapidly as possible. Speed of operation was important and these trains were given track priority. If there were no deliveries or pickups, it was not unusual to have the train roar by the town at full speed. How impressive it was to be within a few yards of the track at the railroad station as these behemoths surged by, steam spewing, smoke billowing, whistle blowing, boxcars squealing, tracks clanking, break shoes scraping, couplers rattling, and dirt flying!

The switchers were dedicated to serving the local communities. These trains were placed on the siding to wait while a high priority train passed by in either direction. Their

Meet My Waterloo   *Trains*

locomotives were put to work during their wait time, and were responsible for distributing boxcars to local businesses and collecting cars. Some of those collected would be added to its own train, while others were assembled for the long-haul freighters to move.

The last category consisted primarily of passenger trains that would stop at every community with a train station, and were nicknamed "milk runs." The trains typically would have a postal service car for the distribution and collection of mail destined for the towns or central post office.

For a young man looking for excitement, the switchers were the best. We would wander along the tracks inspecting the locomotives, and could even talk with the engineer, fireman, or brakeman. They would move along the locomotive's drive wheels with a longneck oil-can, strategically poking its beak into small recesses to feed them oil -- **KERPLUNK KERPLUNK**.

Of course, the train men knew why we were hanging around. Before long we would ask "Can we ride with you while you switch the cars?" The answer was usually a friendly but firm, "No, we're not allowed to give rides," but occasionally we would find a softie who could remember his youthful romance with trains, and we would hitch a ride.

The engineer climbed up the steps into the cab first. He turned to watch us and said, "Come on up." It was a surprise how far apart the steps were (they were farther apart for kids than for grown-ups), but you could not indicate that you had a problem lest the offer would disappear. Once up in the cab, amazement set in regarding the layout and complexity of the operations room called the cab.

On either side of the cab, there were windows facing the front and side, with a seat next to each window. The brakeman sat on one side, the engineer on the other. At the engineer's position, two huge levers reached all the way to the floor, one to determine the train's forward and backward motion, the other, its speed. At the brakeman's position, additional huge levers reached the floor and were used to control the steam for the braking system of the locomotive and trailing freight cars.

A huge firebox occupied the space between the two positions. The immense cast-iron furnace had pipes, valves, and gauges at various locations relating to steam pressure, water level, and myriad other essential measurements necessary for the operation of the locomotive. Almost every gauge had a section marked in red; and seeing that was when you realized that not only were you on a big beast, but a potentially dangerous one also. Centered on the cab, near the floor, was the door to the firebox that permitted the fireman to shovel coal into the fire. He opened the door for us to see inside and we reeled in surprise as the white hot heat of the furnace baked our faces. It was like peering through a hole to Hell. We were glad when he closed the door.

Forward from the firebox was the huge steam chamber. This chamber extended from the firebox and consisted of the entire front end of the steam engine. The steam chamber was an enormous tank positioned on its side and carried by huge drive wheels on either side of the boiler. The firebox heated the water to form steam. Near the front of the boiler section, there were two piston chambers, one on either side of the train. Steam was released to these chambers which in turn drove pistons that were connected to the huge drive wheels. This boiler chamber dominated the steam engine in such a manner

Meet My Waterloo   *Trains*

that the engineer and brakeman sitting in the cab at the rear of the boiler chamber could each see one-half of the scene in front of them. The brakeman would therefore watch for activity on his side of the train, and the engineer would watch for activity on the other.

The rear of the cab was open. A canvas tarpaulin could be drawn across the back, but it was probably used only in winter. The rear of the cab was actually the front of the tender car. Coal was stored in the front of the tender so that the fireman could access the coal to shovel it into the firebox. The locomotive and tender were separate vehicles held together by a coupler. The floor of the cab extended over the top of the floor of the tender so that the fireman could not fall between the two.

The separate and overlapping floor surfaces became apparent as the train was in motion. Each unit of the train "dances" on its springs with its own rhythm due to the irregularities in the rails and track bed. This is true for the locomotive and tender as well, and we watched the fireman nimbly skip across the active divide to fill his shovel at the tender, and return to the firebox door time after time. And we, as "passengers," held onto the cab superstructure to merely stay upright!

There is a mystical difference between the locomotive at rest and one in motion. When the engine is stationary, there are sounds from its innards that make you aware that it is alive. **CLUNK-CLUNK** ----------------**HISS** -----**CLUNK-CLUNK**------------- **HISS**.......... the heartbeat of a resting monster that is ready to spring. You could feel the vibration of the cab floor through your feet, hear it with your ears, and even feel it through your fingers as you hung on to the side.

"**TOOT TOOT.**" We're going to move! The engineer shoved the throttle, and with only light loads to move, the locomotive immediately lurched forward. All the subtle sounds of the motionless train were swamped by the hissing, whooshing, chugging sounds of the pistons driving the wheels, and by the steam-aided draft of the smokestack that belched both white steam and black smoke. **HUSH------------------------------------
---HUSH-------------------------HUSH---------HUSH---------
HUSH--------HUSH----HUSH--HUSHHUSHHUSHHUSH.**
The locomotive bounced and swayed down the track as it gathered speed, jostling the cab and its passengers. The wind whipped into the open rear of the cab carrying with it tiny bits of soot and unburned coal, and we passengers at the rear of the cab suddenly looked like miners with soiled faces, hands, and clothes. What a badge of honor!

After a few episodes of fetching and positioning boxcars, the engineer would swivel on his seat to look at us with our grimy, grinning, faces, and he knew that he had given us the thrill of a lifetime and we had had enough for this outing. He would stop the locomotive, thank us for our interest, inform us that this was the end of the ride, and gently remind us that we had to keep him out of trouble. We promised faithfully to keep quiet, and until you read this account, I have not told the story. Neither the railroad men nor the railroad are around anymore, but I feel they would be thrilled to know that these adventures are now being shared with you.

<u>The Mail</u>
On some trains, there was a mail car used by the U.S. Postal Service. Each day our local post office would bundle mail destined for places other than our town into sturdy canvas sacks. The sacks were taken to the train station to be "shipped" to St. Louis where the mail was sorted for transportation to the

Meet My Waterloo   *Trains*

appropriate destinations. Mail destined for our town was similarly packaged for the mail train's delivery to us. The mail car was attached to a passenger train that rarely stopped at our town, and therefore, pick up and delivery of the mail required special handling.

For mail that was to be picked up at our town, a harness was fastened to the sack and hung from a metal pole alongside the railroad track. The harness had a huge loop through which the speeding train could insert a hook. The bag was then grabbed in much the same way as one could spear the brass ring at the carousel. As the train continued on its way, you could see the arm, mail bag attached, being retracted into the mail car.

For mail being delivered to Waterloo, the process was much simpler. The sack was merely thrown out of the mail car as it passed the station. The station master would warn anyone standing outside, "Heads up" as the train tossed its load at high speed.

Streamliners
While in grade school, we received a student oriented newspaper called the *Weekly Reader*. This paper contained news stories for children at each specific grade level. We were required to read all the stories because there was also a test that accompanied the paper, to help the teacher assess our comprehension. One specific story that I remember was my first encounter with the concept of a "streamliner." This article described a new kind of train engine that was being used on high-speed passenger trains between major cities like Chicago and New York. A careful reading of the story, however, led to the discovery that these streamliner engines were nothing more than steam engines covered with an aerodynamically

Meet My Waterloo *Trains*

shaped metallic skin. They did not fool me! That was still my favorite engine although it had a different suit of clothes.

During the course of World War II, other engines, including diesel and gasoline, were substantially improved and made more economical. It was then I learned that there was a new generation of streamliner being developed that used a diesel powered combustion engine, turning a generator, which in turn powered electric motors on each drive wheel of the locomotive. These new streamliner engines used diesel fuel instead of coal, required no water, did not need a tender, and, even more significantly, could be used in tandem so that multiple units could be driven by one engineer. No more would we hear the **HUSH---HUSH---HUSH** of the steam engine, but instead, the low and continuous **HUMMMMMMMMMMM** of the diesel motor. Instead of the shrill steam whistle, we would now hear the blast of an air horn. Without the need for water, we would no longer hear the clanking of the tender car or hiss of water. How unromantic!

I clearly remember seeing my first streamliner. The town was abuzz with the news that the Gulf, Mobile, and Ohio Railroad was going to put a streamliner on the St. Louis to Mobile, Alabama passenger run. This train came through our town at about seven o'clock in the evening. Our whole family went to the train station to see this new phenomenon. During its introduction, the railroad company had the train stop at each town along its route to show the communities the railroad's progress. We could hear the blast of the air horn announcing the grade crossing north of town. Soon we could see the engine coming down the main track towards the railroad station. All you could hear was the steady hum of the diesel engine. Then, as it approached the station, we could finally see what a radical difference there would be in our notion of train

Meet My Waterloo   *Trains*

travel. The streamliner was totally sheathed in a sleek metallic overcoat to protect its diesel engine, the generator, and the engineer's position. Unlike the steam engines, the streamliner was controlled by the engineer sitting at the very front of the locomotive. Through his windshield, he had a clear view of the tracks in front of him. Each car of the passenger train was specifically designed so that the entire train had a uniform style. How elegant this train seemed with its Pullman cars, its passenger compartments, and the dining car. But no caboose!

This introduction to the train was at once disheartening and disappointing. While there were sounds of awe from many, there was little indication that you had a powerful machine. The mystery of the steam engine was missing. How different the future runs for this train would be. Since this particular passenger train was designated as a "through train," it stopped at our town only when necessary. Therefore many of the subsequent runs would roar into town and rush by the train station. When you viewed the train, the primary effect was to be aware of its high speed and the dirt, dust, and gravel that was thrown up by the rush of air from underneath the cars. This dirty old train was going to replace my precious steam engines! While it took some time, the diesel engine eventually replaced all of the steam engines for freight as well as passenger trains. Little did we know at that time that the airplane would replace most passenger trains, and that many of the train routes would be abandoned. The railroad tracks, water tower, and all sidings have disappeared from Waterloo, and the train station eventually became a restaurant. So much for progress.

The Surprise Airplane Adventure

Chapter 22   Airplanes

When I was very young, seeing any aircraft was rare since they were few in number, and had no established routes to channel them near you. At the sound of an engine, we would race out of the house to see this phenomenon. My earliest recollections of airplanes were of the biplanes. I recall a "pay-per-ride" plane landing south of town near Breezy Hill, and I saw that plane make frequent trips over the town with its passengers. How I envied them!

Gradually, we began to see more planes of various types. Most were single engine aircraft, some with a high wing design, some with a low wing, and a few of the biplanes still remained. Less frequently, but impressively, came the multi-engine planes, and these were amazing to see -- it was hard to understand how something so big could stay aloft. Advertisements started appearing in papers and magazines

Meet My Waterloo   *Airplanes*

showing passengers in these planes, and one wondered how it felt to be up there.

In the late 1930s, a new navigation process was begun. Beacon lights were installed along prescribed routes to guide the aircraft. The beacons were mounted on a high tower that supported a rotating light. The light was focussed to produce a narrow white beam, and the back of the light had a green translucent lens. At night one would see this thin stream of light rotating about the tower, and then see the flash of white light as it scanned the sky directly overhead from your position. When the light was pointed away from your location, a green blink would be seen.

The beacons had multiple purposes. First, they were located on prescribed routes, and separated by approximately twenty to twenty-five miles. A pilot could sequentially fly from beacon to beacon knowing he was on the sky highway. More importantly, the routes could be flown at night with the beacon guiding the plane to illuminated landing fields. Each beacon was next to a flat field that a farmer would deliberately cultivate with low growing plants, or even grass, so that each beacon provided proximity to a small emergency landing field as well.

One such beacon was located north of Waterloo near Gall and HH Roads. In the evening, you could sit in the front yard and see the "flash" created by the beam passing overhead on its three-times-a-minute schedule. From the upstairs of our house, you could see not only the beam, but the green blink as well. Once this navigation aid was installed and operational, we saw many more planes, since both commercial and private pilots were grateful to have this trusty system assist their crude instrumentation. We occasionally rode our bicycles to this

Meet My Waterloo *Airplanes*

beacon and I recall that on the first trip, we were surprised to see how high the tower was, and how small the light. And it operated during the day as well. Daylight flashes were much less noticeable, but present nevertheless as full time markers. Our hope, of course, in visiting the beacon was that some plane might need to land and we would get to see one first hand. No such luck!

I loved the idea of flying, and as a child, enjoyed building the flyable balsa wood model airplanes. That is as close to flying as I expected to get, unless you include the cherry tree. The raw supplies that came with each kit consisted of printed balsa wood sheets that you cut for the complex shapes, balsa sticks for the struts, and paper to cover the model's skeleton. Accessory parts for flying included a propeller, rubber band "motor," and wheels. The models I could afford were for fixed flight, that is, all the control surfaces were rigid, and you had little control of the flight's destiny. One could glue the rudder in a slightly altered position to cause the plane to fly in circles, but that was the limit of your control over the fight path. You wound up the rubber band motor by cranking the propeller backwards, then released the model, hoping for the best. How many times the flight ended in a crash because of some warped surface, wrong gust of wind, or turn into a tree or bush. Glue and patch paper were constant companions during flight attempts. But how exhilarating when the model soared into a good wind, and flew a great distance beyond your expectations! One good flight like that erased the disappointments derived from prior catastrophes.

One day, a small aircraft was heard flying over the field in back of our house, and it sounded very low. I ran out to investigate, and to my amazement, as it approached Columbia Avenue on its way north, the engine noise ceased. The plane

Meet My Waterloo   *Airplanes*

slowly disappeared behind trees lining the street. I ran full speed towards the airplane, as did every other kid from the north side of Waterloo. When I arrived, I saw the plane sitting in the field. It was a small, tandem seat, high wing, canvas covered plane called a Piper J-3. It had big balloon tires to enable it to land on rough fields. It was surprising to me how small the plane was. The pilot was nowhere in sight, and I was told he retrieved a gas can from the rear of the aircraft and started walking to the highway to get resupplied.

The side window to the pilot's compartment was open. The entire window was hinged on the bottom, and it rested against the side of the airplane. I approached the vehicle to see what a real plane looked like on the inside, and the temptation to experiment was irresistible. I reached through the window and grabbed the "stick," the primary attitude control for the aircraft, and began moving it. Moving it right or left, the surfaces on the edges of the wings rose or fell in opposition to each other (to govern the plane's tilt when in flight). Moving the stick forward or backwards made the surfaces on the rear elevator rise or fall in unison (controlling the climb or descent of the plane). So this is how it worked! You could even see the thin cables leading to the control surfaces. The floor pedals were connected by wires to the rudder, but I did not dare climb in the plane to test that action lest the pilot return and catch me in the act. But I had touched a real plane, and was it exciting! Now I really wanted to fly. I waited for a long time for the pilot to return so I could see him take off (a ride?). But the 6:00 P.M. siren sounded, announcing mandatory attendance at supper, and I had to leave. How I wanted to disobey just this once!

During a summer vacation, I stayed several weeks with Uncle Wilbur in St. Louis. One evening, he took me to Lambert

Field to watch the commercial planes land and take off. On top of the airport's single hanger was the rotating beacon signifying it was on the air route. It was thrilling to watch the huge aircraft take off and land early in the evening. Most of the events were landings because there was very little night flying then, and therefore few departures near dusk. Later in the evening as it became dark, and landings were still needed, a new process took place. There were no runway lights, however there was a search light that would track the landing aircraft and illuminate the runway area near the plane. To keep from blinding the pilot, a column of smoke was created at the searchlight to develop a vertical shadow. This shadow was placed directly in line with the pilot. Selective lighting! This was real science.

The following Sunday, Wilbur took me back, and signed us up for a local flight. Unfortunately, the pilot made me sit in the back seat of the four "seater" plane, while designating my uncle to sit up front next to him. I was sufficiently small, that, when buckled in, I could barely see the horizon over the bottom edge of the side window, and could see what was below the plane only when it banked during a turn. Even worse, the motor made so much noise that no one could hear my questions and complaints. And, to my surprise, air is bumpy. The little plane bobbed and swayed to each distinct pocket of air. This was not the fun I anticipated! But, having been up, I had bragging rights back home.

As the 1940s materialized, the planes changed again and sightings became more frequent. Movies introduced us to the World War II fighters and bombers, and air warden guides showed the actual shapes of friendly and unfriendly aircraft in profile. And one could tell there was a new generation of planes from their sound. The engines sounded more powerful

Meet My Waterloo   *Airplanes*

and the slurring (Doppler effect) of their sound as they passed overhead changed more quickly, showing they were very fast. We would rush outside when we heard one or more of these beauties. Look! P-41s, or a P-39, or a P-50. And there were bombers, B-17s and B-25s. These planes would pass by, sometimes in formation, and how impressive the sight! Daily sightings of DC-3s were common, since they were now being used as military as well as commercial transports. There was no question that war was causing a large growth in flight capability.

And then the beacons disappeared, or rather, were turned off. We no longer had our nighttime beam, I suppose to thwart the enemy, or perhaps we had better guidance now.

Shortly after the war ended, one of the young men that had served as a pilot in the service bought a surplus training plane. This was a silver, low wing, monoplane with a glassed in cockpit area. How thrilling to see acrobatics for the first time! Summer afternoons were frequently appointed with big fluffy cumulus clouds, and he would fly that plane in, around, under, over and through these clouds as if playing Hide-and-Seek with an imaginary companion. Loops and rolls were part of his repertoire, as was the stall. He would point the plane skyward, while reducing the engine's power. Soon the plane would cease to climb, and fall over in a spin with the only sound the whistle of wind past some plane surface. The sun flashed from various parts of the aircraft as it twirled downward. Then, as he approached the ground, this pilot's engine would roar to life, the plane would stop spinning, and the craft would gently swoop back into the sky. This maneuver was even more impressive and mysterious when executed above the clouds. You knew what was happening, but could not see the action until the plane broke under the cloud cover. Oh, how I wanted

<u>*Meet My Waterloo*</u>   <u>*Airplanes*</u>

to fly like that -- to be able to soar through the clouds -- to have the whole sky as my playground!

**Part VIII
Vocation**

Chapter 23 Growing Up

The Delivery Boy

Chapter 23   Growing Up

Each child was taught that work was part of living. Responsibilities were dispensed commensurate with your age. Quality performance was expected, and your accomplishments were judged. A task assigned at one age did not give way to more complex ones as you got older -- they were added. Therefore, when you were very young, your job was to carry kindling to the basement, and as you got older, chopping the kindling was added. Likewise, carrying away the grass cuttings was just the precursor to mowing as well.

Until you were ten or eleven years old, work was mostly for your own family. Later, neighbors solicited your services, and you were paid consistent with your age, not the work. Therefore, when I began mowing lawns for hire, I was paid the apprentice wage the first year, and the experienced wage thereafter, even though the work was the same. Since there was competition in lawn mowing, the buyer had control.

When I was old enough to ride my bicycle on the public highway, I joined my friends in the summertime job of tomato picking. We would meet in the mornings, and ride north on Route 3 to a farm near the Country Club. Work began around nine o'clock. Each person picked two rows of tomatoes at a time, and placed the fruit in a hamper.

Tomatoes are nearly all water, and the hamper soon became very heavy. Once it was full, you had to lug the hamper back to the beginning of the row so that another crew could place the hampers on a truck. The farmer would inspect your pickings as you delivered the hampers, checking that you picked only large and ripe fruit. Work was paid by the hamper, but full value was paid only if the product delivered was acceptable.

Illinois summer days are brutally hot, and by ten o'clock, one could be wet with sweat. Additionally, tomato vines are covered with a prickly layer that itched when it rubbed against your skin. Occasionally, one would accidentally pick a rotten tomato, and the stench would add to your misery. It became even worse if, through boredom, one of your compatriots mischievously hit you with a rotten tomato, and now this liquid stewed on your clothes in the hot sun. This work for pay was no fun, and would have been unbearable if it were not accomplished in the company of friends. At the end of the work day, we would ride home together competing again with the Route 3 traffic. Once at home, you stripped off your work clothes in the basement and then took a bath to escape that tomato smell.

Meet My Waterloo   *Growing Up*

Each day, one would pick in a different field, or different portion of a prior day's field. Within several days, a new crop of tomatoes would be ready on the first vines, and the process would be repeated. The season lasted about four weeks and a sizable amount of money (for a kid) could be earned. And not every day was totally under that oppressive sun. On some days, an afternoon thunderstorm would roll through, and we relished the cool rain. While our shoes usually became muddy, the rain soaking into our clothes was refreshing, and the farmer would let us continue to pick unless there was danger from lightning.

Not all work was for pay -- some was for patriotism. During the war, scrap drives would be held to collect old iron, steel, and copper. One did get paid, but in war stamps or bonds, and it was unheard of to cash these during the conflict. I would clean out garages, basements, attics, and old barns for the privilege of retaining any materials useful to the effort. And the process was successful. I had a mound of scrap in our yard that was the blight of the neighborhood! But all for a good cause, and regularly, the "scrap truck" would come and pick up the mound. The weight of the load was determined by using the flour mill truck scale, and you were paid in war stamps. These were promptly pasted into your savings book. Of course, a fringe benefit to this patriotic effort was that I kept the old radios for my hobby activities in the shed.

But all this work for pay was sporadic and usually limited my income to the summer time. My first "grown up" job came as a Saturday grocery delivery boy working for Rau's Grocery. Earl ("Curly") Rau had been called into the service, and his wife Coralyn took over running the store. She not only managed the store, but was the butcher! She also had two clerks, both wives of service men. Nelda, one of the clerks, was primarily responsible for supervising the deliveries.

On Saturdays, a customer could call in an order by telephone and it would be filled and delivered that day. I was hired as the "delivery boy." The title was a misnomer; I could not drive, so I was the helper who carried the boxes.

The telephone order was written by hand into the grocery receipt book. Nelda separately transcribed the meat cutting requirements and gave them to Coralyn who would fill the order. Meat orders were placed in the refrigerator until the delivery trip was ready to go. Nelda and I would each take a list, and fill empty packing boxes with the items ordered. These boxes were placed on the floor near the front of the store. The route would be planned to minimize driving, and I would shuffle the boxes to be consistent with the plan. After the refrigerated products were added, I would carry the boxes to the delivery car.

Vehicles were nearly impossible to get during the war, and therefore the deliveries were made using Coralyn's standard two-door sedan. The boxes were stacked carefully to maximize the load. Maneuvering those heavy boxes in and out of the two-door sedan was hard work, therefore the last order to be delivered was always the first in the car so it could be on the bottom, and the remaining orders followed a similar sequencing. It was not uncommon that the first order to be delivered sat on my lap as we started our rounds.

At each stop, I would carry the food stuffs into the buyer's home. For those that did not want the boxes, I would unload the goods onto the kitchen table while Nelda handled the money and food stamp transactions.

Four pouches were used to keep track of the payments. One pouch, of course, was for money, and the remainder for the rationing scrip. Separate sacks were required for red stamps and tokens (meat), blue stamps and tokens (canned goods), and special stamps (sugar). Nelda handled most of these transactions, but after a while, I was gradually "broken in" to the "business" side of the operation. I got to know the customers, and they, me. And it was flattering to be recognized as an "almost" grown up.

As I became more adept at this work, and customers became accustomed to me, Nelda and I would split deliveries at those stops where two customers lived very close together. I would carry Nelda's order, then leave and carry "my" customer's order. For this process, I had my own money and stamp pouches. Another dose of "grown up."

Stop after stop would be made along the planned route, then, back to the store for another car full of deliveries. This work consumed a large portion of the day, and you had to hustle because customers did not want deliveries late in the afternoon. After the final "run," we would retreat to the store, and reconcile our transaction pouches against the orders delivered. The money, red stamps, blue stamps, and specials all had to balance against that required in "payment" on the order sheet. Money was, of course important; however, to get resupplied with rationed goods, the store had to exchange stamps with the distributors, so accuracy in the stamp transactions was vital also. Now I was also becoming a bookkeeper.

The remainder of my day was allocated to chores. Cleaning up the delivery car and flattening the delivery boxes completed the "delivery boy" tasks. During the day, the distributor's truck would deliver cases of foodstuffs to the store, and these he stacked by the back door. My job was to get the stack out of the doorway by placing designated cases of goods on the shelves, and then carrying the remainder downstairs to the store room. Then, sweep the store, burn the boxes, and it was PAYDAY! How good it felt to have earned that reward and have steady employment!

Epilog

The End of One Era, The Beginning of the New

By the end of summer in 1945, I knew that I had reached the end of one phase of my development, and change was on the horizon. In May, I had been confirmed by my church and was now considered a member of the congregation. (Now the sermons were for me as well.) Then, I graduated from eighth grade, and high school was a new beckoning experience. The Depression was a thing of the past, and money and jobs were available. In May, the war in Europe ended, in July, we tested a new kind of bomb in New Mexico, and by August, the war in the Pacific ceased. Instead of roaming the town for free excitement, I was serving the town as a delivery boy -- for pay.

PLAYTIME WAS OVER, ON TO THE NEXT ADVENTURE.

My church, in order to encourage intra-denominational friendship between the young but confirmed boys and girls, had a social group called the Walther League. The express purpose was to continue Christian fellowship within the younger generation through a little bit of teaching and a lot of fun together. This fun included such activities as treasure hunts, hay rides, and sometimes an evening of games. Often, we went to the Water Works where we spent a little time in discussion, then played games, and rounded out the time with cookies and pop or a marshmallow roast. On one of the first of such outings after we had become eligible through Confirmation, we were introduced to a variation of an old game. The girls formed an inner ring, the boys, the outer, with a boy directly behind each girl. When chosen, the boy-girl combination had to race around the outside of the circle in a race against another couple. In order to get a better start, it was appropriate for the boy to place his hands at the girl's waist.

OH WOW!!!! GIRLS ARE SOFT!!!!

Endnotes

[1] *The Waterloo Republican,* February 2, 1955

[2] Cahokia Mounds Historic Site Visitor's Brochure

[3] Waterloo Chamber of Commerce Brochure

[4] Recording company and composer unknown, believed to have been sung by The Andrew Sisters, circa 1939.

[5] Our house, as well most of the other houses built in the 1920's had indoor plumbing. Why then the outhouse? It was the age of transition. Homes before about 1910 did not have indoor plumbing, and therefore those who grew up during that time were reconciled to the outhouse. Those even older, expected it. People who built homes in the 1920s still had acquaintances not accustomed to the new contraptions. Therefore, both facilities were installed.

About the Author

Lloyd Engelbrecht was born in Chicago in 1931 and moved downstate to Waterloo three years later. He graduated from Waterloo High School with strong interest in both art and science. He earned his degree in electrical engineering from the University of Illinois Champaign-Urbana in 1953. After military service from 1953 through 1955, he began his forty-two year career as a communication engineer, while earning the additional degrees of MSEE from the Illinois Institute of Technology and MBA from the University of Santa Clara. Twelve patents bear his name as inventor. In 1997, he began his second career as an artist in several media including photography, acrylic-on-canvas painting, and paper sculpture. Drawing on his writing experience from his engineering past, he has also become an author, documenting his life's experiences. He is married to Molly Hurlbut Engelbrecht, and they make their home at The Sea Ranch in California.

www.ingramcontent.com/pod-product-compliance
Lightning Source LLC
Chambersburg PA
CBHW072133160426
43197CB00012B/2082